A DAY IN THE LIFE OF A
STUDENT AFFAIRS EDUCATOR

A DAY IN THE LIFE

OF A STUDENT

AFFAIRS EDUCATOR

Competencies and Case Studies for Early-Career Professionals

Sarah M. Marshall and
Anne M. Hornak

Foreword by Susan R. Komives

STERLING, VIRGINIA

Published by Stylus Publishing, LLC
22883 Quicksilver Drive
Sterling, Virginia 20166-2102

Library of Congress Cataloging-in-Publication Data
Marshall, Sarah M., 1971-
A day in the life of a student affairs educator : competencies and case
studies for early career professionals / Sarah M. Marshall and Anne
M. Hornak ; foreword by Susan R. Komives. – First edition.
  pages cm
Includes bibliographical references and index.
ISBN 978-1-57922-308-3 (cloth : alk. paper)
ISBN 978-1-57922-309-0 (pbk. : alk. paper)
ISBN 978-1-62036-212-9 (consumer e-edition)
ISBN 978-1-62036-211-2 (library e-edition)
1. Student affairs services–United States–Administration–Case
studies. 2. Student affairs administrators–United States–Case
studies. I. Hornak, Anne M., 1972- II. Title.
LB2343.M36 2014
371.4–dc23
                                                        2014015241
13-digit ISBN: 978-1-57922-308-3 (cloth)
13-digit ISBN: 978-1-57922-309-0 (paperback)
13-digit ISBN: 978-1-62036-211-2 (library networkable e-edition)
13-digit ISBN: 978-1-62036-212-9 (consumer e-edition)

Printed in the United States of America

All first editions printed on acid-free paper
that meets the American National Standards Institute
Z39-48 Standard.

Bulk Purchases

Quantity discounts are available for use in workshops and for
staff development.
Call 1-800-232-0223

First Edition, 2014

10   9   8   7   6   5   4   3   2

CONTENTS

FOREWORD

The Airline Philosophy of Professional Life

Susan R. Komives

Things that happen to us do not become experience without reflection.

—David A. Kolb

I can assert with confidence that there is probably not a single student affairs professional who has not said, "They could make a fascinating TV series out of my life—one episode an inspiring drama, the next a comedy, the next a tragedy, and a soap opera; all with a great ensemble cast!" The stories behind each of the case studies in *A Day in the Life of a Student Affairs Educator* could provide the scripts of a great show!

However, watching a TV series—or even reading a well-crafted case study—may not mean any learning is happening! But when intentionally used, it can be an inductive learning experience. From the context presented, one has to sort the important actions from the trivial to make meaning and to learn from the experience. A case study used in a group professional development setting is an active experience of seeking understanding and meaning with others, rehearsing possible courses of action, and perhaps even knowing how the "real" case turned out. Kolb's (1984; Kolb & Kolb, 2005) model of experiential learning comes to life in studying the *concrete experience* of the case. The *reflection* that follows makes meaning and adds understanding, followed by the *abstract conceptualization* of what might be done and why, then the *active experimentation* of planning a new approach or an intervention and seeing how that goes. Mastering the thoughtful process of this *What?–So What?–Now What?* cycle is an essential professional competency in itself.

The authors of this publication were wise to organize the case studies in the framework of the 10 Professional Competency Areas for Student Affairs Practitioners developed jointly by the American College Personnel Association (ACPA) and NASPA—Student Affairs Administrators in Higher Education (2010). The pedagogical utility of this organization is superb and will allow for targeted use in staff development programming and for individuals who seek to challenge their own development through the complexity of the basic, intermediate, and advanced levels of each competency. When well developed, cases can promote higher-order thinking like applying, analyzing, evaluating, or creating (Krathwohl, 2002). I would encourage all users to develop their own case studies practicing the highest order of complexity: creating!

I was certainly very pleased when ACPA and NASPA invited the Council for the Advancement of Standards in Higher Education (CAS) to participate in the competency project and it was my pleasure to serve on this group as the CAS President. I want to call attention to three common threads that members of the Joint Task Force on Professional Competencies and Standards felt were woven throughout all 10 competencies: technology, sustainability, and globalism. Today's professional should be competent in how dimensions of each of those threads shape and are shaped by each of the 10 competency areas. I would also note that although ethical professional practice is its own competency area, I think every case study analysis should include the question, Is this an ethical issue?; and, if it is, participants should turn to the ACPA and/or NASPA ethical guides to assist with this analysis.

Each time you settle into your seat on an airplane, the flight attendant admonishes passengers that if the oxygen mask is released, you should put the mask on yourself first and then help the person next to you. Developing yourself is so critical that the 10 competencies were created with three layers of developmental complexity, and that personal foundations is one of the competencies. Developing yourself to be the best professional you can be is critical to quality programs and services for your students and your institution. Developing yourself is a lifelong quest; it is a journey without end; it is a commitment to the humble awareness that you can always be better at what is important. Enjoy this book on your personal journey.

REFERENCES

ACPA & NASPA. (2010). *ACPA/NASPA professional competency areas for student affairs practitioners*. Washington, DC: Authors.

Kolb, D.A. (1984). *Experiential learning: Experiences as the source of learning and development*. Englewood Cliffs, NJ: Prentice-Hall.

Kolb, A.Y., & Kolb, D. A. (2005). Learning styles and learning spaces: Enhancing experiential learning in higher education. *Academy of Management Learning & Education*, 4(2), 193–212.

Krathwohl, D. R. (2002). A revision of Bloom's taxonomy: An overview. *Theory Into Practice, 41*(4), 212–218.

Susan R. Komives is professor emerita from the student affairs graduate program at the University of Maryland. A former president of ACPA and CAS, she was a member of the team that developed the ACPA/NASPA professional competencies. She is the recipient of the ACPA 2012 Lifetime Achievement Award.

ACKNOWLEDGMENTS

We are most thankful to the students and administrators who took time out of their busy schedules to share their stories and cases with us. Your insights and honesty framed these cases and will aid in the development of many student affairs professionals in the future.

We are blessed to have the love and support of our families. For Sarah, she is forever grateful for the love, encouragement, and championing from her partner, Dave. Her daughters, Lauren and Anna Grace, provided their humor, love, patience, and inquisitiveness regarding her writing. For Anne, she is grateful for the unconditional love and support from her partner, David. Her daughter, Olivia, and son, Maxwell, have been a joy in their encouragement and curiosity throughout the writing and crafting of the cases.

We are both grateful to Jenifer Witt for her tireless editing, compiling, and organizing of cases and chapters as we moved through the process. She was always willing to help even with ambiguous and obscure directives. We also acknowledge the contributions of Kay Harris, who worked early in the process on the editing and compiling of cases.

Finally, we wish to thank our colleagues at Central Michigan University for their support throughout this process. Their willingness to allow us to use the cases in our courses as well as to provide honest and constructive feedback was invaluable.

A *Day in the Life of a Student Affairs Educator: Competencies and Case Studies for Early-Career Professionals* is a collection of case studies exploring issues facing new professionals in student affairs and higher education. The case study scenarios in this book are organized around the Professional Competency Areas for Student Affairs Practitioners developed jointly by the American College Personnel Association (ACPA) and NASPA—Student Affairs Administrators in Higher Education (NASPA) (ACPA & NASPA, 2010). The chapters include: advising and helping; assessment, evaluation, and research; equity, diversity, and inclusion; ethical professional practice; history, philosophy, and values; human and organizational resources; law, policy, and governance; leadership; personal foundations; and student learning and development. The cases within each area vary in length to allow for multiple uses. Shorter cases can be role-played and discussed in leadership training workshops, while longer cases can be take-home assignments or debated during longer training sessions. Additionally, at the end of the book, we offer general advice from current professionals in the field.

NEED FOR THIS BOOK

The need to create meaningful learning experiences for students has long been the goal for many faculty and student affairs professionals as they design courses, facilitate training programs, and mentor new professionals. True learning experiences are situations where students and professionals can make meaning of information and learn to process it within their own contexts.

Ideally, in these learning situations, students ask themselves, "How does this impact my life and work?" Baxter Magolda (2001) says, "preparing students for life after college requires engaging their minds and their internal selves to work toward the complexity they will need for success" (p. 326). Providing opportunities for students to analyze real-life case studies is an invaluable way to engage both their minds and internal selves. This extends beyond the classroom into ongoing professional development. Student affairs is a dynamic and ever-changing profession, and as ethical leaders their keeping current is critical to staying connected.

> Students learn more when they are intensely involved in their education and have opportunities to think about and apply what they are learning in different settings. Furthermore, when students collaborate with others in solving problems or mastering difficult material, they acquire valuable skills that prepare them to deal with messy, unscripted problems they will encounter daily during and after college. (Kuh, Kinzie, Schuh, Whitt, & Associates, 2005, p. 193)

Case studies provide the opportunity to become intensely involved in the material and to analyze and discuss issues and problems student affairs professionals face daily. In addition, Baxter Magolda (2001) found that when students are actively and collaboratively working together, the opportunities to construct and co-construct knowledge take on deeper meaning and have more application to their own experiences. We also see these cases as excellent training tools for new and mid-level professionals. The need to be immersed in conflicting and dysfunctional structure problems provides a rich learning tool.

In conversations with new professionals, time and time again, professionals relayed how little training they received before assuming their leadership and, many times, supervisory positions. Most learned by trial and error, others may have received an out-of-date officer binder, and a few got advice from the previous professional. We believe that the meaningful dialogue generated by analyzing these cases can serve as a powerful professional development tool for new and mid-level professionals. It is our intent that individuals learn from the examples and discuss the courses of action before they actually encounter them in real life. These cases provide an excellent opportunity to role-play and discuss scenarios before they play out in their daily lives.

METHODOLOGY AND ORGANIZATION

The cases included in this collection stem from interviews with current student affairs professionals. They are based on real-life dilemmas and reflect many contemporary and historical issues on our college campuses. The interviews also ground us in the current roles administrators play on our campuses. While we realize that our college and university campuses vary in hierarchy and structure, our goal is to make the case studies broad enough to apply across the diversity of higher education. Throughout the process we talked to 126 student affairs administrators, in both group settings and one-on-one interviews. The interviews were conducted at 11 different colleges and universities in four states in the Midwest. The schools included large public research institutions; small private colleges; community colleges; and mid-size, comprehensive schools.

The book is laid out in chapter format, with each chapter representing cases categorized around the ACPA/NASPA competencies; some cases fall under multiple competencies. Those cases are found in the chapter most closely linked with the competency; however, at the end of this introduction there is a table listing the cases organized across the competency areas (Table I-1). Chapter 2 offers an overview of each competency. Within each chapter you will find a variety of situations germane to the designated competency. Some competencies align themselves more easily to the cases than others; therefore, we have not included an equal number in each chapter.

We recognize that while some dilemmas on our campuses are isolated to just one area (i.e., Greek life, residence life, academic advising), others may cut across divisions; Table 1-2, at the end of this introduction, lists the cases and their relation to different institutional divisions. We offer some cases that relate directly to a particular competency, while others may cross multiple competencies, as the issues affect the broader campus community. In addition, we are aware that student affairs nomenclature varies from campus to campus. We tried to use general terms in describing offices, functional areas, and roles. As you read the cases, please feel free to change the language to relate to your particular campus and any other details that may increase discussion and deepen conversations. Please adapt the case so the terminology is specific to your campus.

The cases vary in length. Some, intentionally, do not offer a lot of detail. We strongly suggest that you encourage students to ad lib any details needed for them to process these cases. As experienced faculty, we have seen many case study facilitations go downhill when the analyzers claim they do not have enough information to process the case. If you feel as if you do not have enough information, embellish, add it, or discuss using "what-if" statements. Use these statements to fill in details to play out the scenario with different factors.

HOW TO USE THIS BOOK

While we anticipate that faculty who may be more experienced in using case studies in their classes will use this book, we also recognize that many users may be student affairs professionals who train newer professionals and facilitate ongoing professional development. Our goal is for readers to use this book as a supplement in graduate training programs as well as training programs for new professionals and across campuses. To assist with the facilitation process, we provide discussion questions to begin the analysis of each case. The cases are written broadly enough to allow for a variety of possible solutions, depending on the students' vantage point and what they deem to be important issues in the case. In this section, we offer advice for the facilitator, summarize the steps in analyzing a case, and conclude with a role-play activity that may be used with students.

We offer you, the facilitator, a few suggestions for discussing these cases effectively. First, we recommend that you review the case before presenting it and identify the questions you want explored. You can use the questions we present or create your own. Second, we suggest that you adapt the cases as necessary so your constituents will understand the terminology and so the case relates to your campus. Third, we strongly suggest that you understand your campus culture, policies, and procedures, and the expectations of your campus leaders, before you jump into case analysis. Knowing the rules that govern your campus is imperative so that the suggestions or advice you provide comply with the guidelines of your college or university. Fourth, if you are unclear about what should be done in a particular case, we suggest you seek the advice of others before presenting it. Fifth, as you are a role model for new professionals and graduate students, it is important that you model appropriate behavior. Sometimes doing the right thing is not the most popular or easy decision. Recognizing the influence your behavior has on these professionals is essential. We encourage you to do the right thing and challenge your colleagues to do the same.

Next, there are some key steps in analyzing a case. We have found that when using case studies, those who review often want to jump to what they would do rather than analyze the key points. We suggest that, as the facilitator, you prevent this premature discussion and use the following steps to facilitate your discussion. To assist you, we include many of these same questions at the end of each case.

First, have the participants discuss the organizational environment relevant to the case. Second, have the participants identify the problem or problems in the case. Individuals often interpret each case differently. Having a clear understanding and agreed-upon central and secondary problems is important to analysis. Third, discuss the key stakeholders for each case. Identifying key people will help students to discuss the possible actions and how each scenario may affect each constituent. Fourth, identify possible courses of action and how each one might play out; this is a critical step in case analysis. Again, many students will opt for a quick solution without properly weighing each possible course of action and its impact.

As you play out each proposed course of action, challenge the students to think about the pros and cons of each idea. What is the potential long- or short-term impact? They should also consider campus policies and procedures, legal constraints, ethical implications, and reactions from various stakeholders. Once they have thoroughly weighed each possible action and its potential consequences, we suggest that you have them select the best scenario. Once they determine the best course of action, have the students draft an implementation plan. When they have completed the case analysis, you should have them reflect on additional questions at the end of the case.

As we mentioned earlier, these cases can be used a variety of ways: they can be assignments for students to take home and prepare written responses to; or they can be read aloud and discussed in larger group settings, smaller breakout groups, or one-on-one. We suggest using these cases at the beginning of the year as part of training. Also, as ongoing professional development, consider reading one case at the beginning of each meeting and then discussing it as a group. This would be a meaningful way to continue training throughout the school year.

Another way to use these case studies is to role-play the scenarios. One technique is to ask for volunteers or assign roles from the case to the students.

Read the case, and then ask the participants to play out the scenario. Give them permission to be creative and let the role-play evolve. A couple of minutes into the role-play, others are allowed to participate by "tapping out" one of the key participants in the role-play. For example, if the case involves a student leader and an advisor, the facilitator assigns each role, and the participants start to play out the scenario. After a given amount of time, as the facilitator, you give a signal that someone observing the role-play may tap out one of the participants. In other words, a member from the audience can approach the scenario while it is in progress, tap one of the actors on the shoulder, and take his or her place in the role-play. The original person then takes a seat, and the new person picks up the role-play where the former player left off. This is an excellent way to involve others and can exemplify how people approach situations differently. Speaking from experience, participants enjoy this activity and appreciate that they can tap into a scenario if they are frustrated with how it is progressing or save someone who is floundering.

USING THE ACPA/NASPA COMPETENCIES

The profession of student affairs is diverse and varied. The profession has struggled to find a common set of values, skills, standards, and competencies that define the work student affair professionals do daily (ACPA & NASPA, 2010; CAS, 2012). The goal has not been to standardize the work professionals do, but rather to provide a common voice to frame the work.

The Council for the Advancement of Standards (CAS) began addressing this issue in the 1970s by developing standards related to student learning outcomes. The work of the organization continues today with the 2012 revised CAS standards. In addition to CAS, ACPA and NASPA pulled together a work group to begin to address the skills, competencies, and knowledge associated with student affairs. The group spent a year reviewing related literature and research, which resulted in the publication, *Professional Competency Areas for Student Affairs Practitioners* (ACPA & NASPA, 2010).

The competencies are intended to provide a baseline for the expected knowledge, skills, and attitudes expected of those working in student affairs.

Student affairs is a unique field in that individuals enter from multiple disciplines and not always through a traditional student affairs or higher education graduate program. Entry into positions in higher education administration and student affairs is often at the master's level, with preparation degrees varying across multiple disciplines. The competencies offer a basic list of outcomes that begin to inform practice, and the cases in this book are arranged into chapters related to these competencies. Within each competency area are three levels: basic, intermediate, and advanced (see Table I-1). The increasing levels are associated with more complex learning outcomes and skills.

The 10 competency areas developed by the joint task force are: advising and helping; assessment, evaluation, and research; equity, diversity, and inclusion; ethical professional practice; history, philosophy, and values; human and organizational resources; law, policy, and governance; leadership; personal foundations; and student learning and development (ACPA & NASPA, 2010). The joint task force also identified three "threads"— technology, sustainability, and globalism—that are embedded throughout most of the competency areas. Rather than having these threads stand alone as separate competency areas, the task force represented them as expected knowledge embedded within each competency. Organizing the cases around the competencies enables participants to analyze their work through multiple skill sets. Individuals working within a functional area use several skills in their work, and the competencies offer a list of outcomes that can cut across functional areas. We have not separated out the threads within the organization of the book; rather, we encourage readers to infuse the threads into their analyses of the cases. We explore the competencies briefly here to offer context for each chapter. The narrative regarding each competency is written verbatim from the text of the ACPA and NASPA (2010) document. Our intention was to stay true to the meaning and goal the authors of the document intended.

Advising and Helping

"The advising and helping competency area addresses the knowledge, skills, and attitudes related to providing counseling and advising support, direction, feedback, critique, referral, and guidance to individuals and groups" (ACPA & NASPA, 2010, p. 8). This competency is classified within a basic, intermediate, and advanced skill set. The levels provide an opportunity to refine the skills and attitudes associated with the advising and helping framework.

Assessment, Evaluation, and Research

"The assessment, evaluation, and research competency area (AER) focuses on the ability to use, design, conduct, and critique qualitative and quantitative AER analyses; to manage organizations using AER processes and the results obtained from them; and to shape the political and ethical climate surrounding AER processes and uses on campus" (ACPA & NASPA, 2010, p. 10).

Assessment, evaluation, and research is critical in student affairs as professionals are required to provide more program assessment and to understand how data are driving decision making and budget allocations.

Equity, Diversity, and Inclusion

"The equity, diversity, and inclusion (EDI) competency area includes the knowledge, skills, and attitudes needed to create learning environments that are enriched with diverse views and people. It is also designed to create an institutional ethos that accepts and celebrates differences among people, helping to free them of any misconceptions and prejudices" (ACPA & NASPA, 2010, p. 12). This is a critical skill set as our campuses and learning environments become more and more diverse.

Ethical Professional Practice

"The ethical professional practice competency area pertains to the knowledge, skills, and attitudes needed to understand and apply ethical standards to one's work. While ethics is an integral component of all the competency areas, this competency area focuses specifically on the integration of ethics into all aspects of self and professional practice" (ACPA & NASPA, 2010, p. 14). The ability of student affairs professionals to identify an ethical dilemma and use sound decision-making skills is critical to the reputation of the institution and the profession.

History, Philosophy, and Values

"The history, philosophy, and values competency area involves knowledge, skills, and attitudes that connect the history, philosophy, and values of the profession to one's current professional practice. This competency area embodies the foundations of the profession from which current and future research and practice will grow. The commitment to demonstrating this competency area ensures that our present and future practices are informed by an understanding of our history, philosophy, and values" (ACPA & NASPA, 2010, p. 16). Practices that are tied to the foundations and tenets of the profession are more effective.

Human and Organizational Resources

"The human and organizational resources competency area includes knowledge, skills, and attitudes used in the selection, supervision, motivation, and formal evaluation of staff; conflict resolution; management of the politics of organizational discourse; and the effective application of strategies and techniques associated with financial resources, facilities management, fundraising, technology use, crisis management, risk management, and sustainable resources" (ACPA & NASPA, 2010, p. 18). The financial costs associated with hiring and retaining professionals is very high. Developing skills that increase effectiveness in using both human and capital resources can maximize efficiency across the organization.

Law, Policy, and Governance

"The law, policy, and governance competency area includes the knowledge, skills, and attitudes relating to policy development processes used in various contexts, the application of legal constructs, and the understanding of governance structures and their effects on one's professional practice" (ACPA & NASPA, 2010, p. 22). This skill set is critical for student affairs professionals as many of the dilemmas they face have legal and policy implications for both students and the institution.

Leadership

"The leadership competency area addresses the knowledge, skills, and attitudes required of a leader, whether it be a positional leader or a member of the staff, in both an individual capacity and within a process of how individuals work together effectively to envision, plan, effect change in organizations, and respond to internal and external constituencies and issues" (ACPA & NASPA, 2010, p. 24). This competency area defines both being a leader and being a member of a team. This is a critical skill for professionals as they climb the career ladder; having a sound leadership style can be as important as being a good follower.

Personal Foundations

"The personal foundations competency area involves the knowledge, skills, and attitudes to maintain emotional, physical, social, environmental, relational, spiritual, and intellectual wellness; be self-directed and self-reflective; maintain excellence and integrity in work; be comfortable with ambiguity; be aware of one's own areas of strength and growth; have a passion for work; and remain curious" (ACPA & NASPA, 2010, p. 26). The area is critical as the burnout rate for new student affairs professionals is high. The need to develop the capacity to understand balance and the commitment to wellness is crucial in the future growth of the profession.

Student Learning and Development

"The student learning and development competency area addresses the concepts and principles of student development and learning theory. This includes the ability to apply theory to improve and inform student affairs practice, as well as understanding teaching and training theory and practice" (ACPA & NASPA, 2010, p. 28). Student affairs professionals who understand the importance of development theory in their practice are more effective. Programs and learning experiences that are grounded in developmentally appropriate theory result in better outcomes for students.

CASES AND ORGANIZATION

The ACPA/NASPA competency areas provide a basic list of outcomes expected of professionals working in student affairs and higher education. The list, organized with basic, intermediate, and advanced outcomes, can aid in designing ongoing professional development opportunities for your students, supervisees, and colleagues, as they desire to grow in certain areas.

We organized the chapters in this book by the competencies; however, we would argue that these cases be analyzed using the theories and developmental foundations associated with student growth. Student development theories also serve an important role in explaining and predicting student behavior. Theories serve as tools in our analysis of student behavior and program development. College students navigate the college terrain academically, socially, morally, and even physically as they negotiate their identities and ask life questions such as, Who am I? Who do I want to be? The theories associated with college students and their development gives us the foundation to explain these behaviors as we develop ongoing professional development opportunities. Additionally, new professionals do not always enter the profession through a student affairs preparation program. Therefore it is critical that, as supervisors and mentors, we challenge new professionals to use theory during the case analysis.

Many times multiple theories can be used in one case for analysis. The goal is to help case study participants find appropriate theories to frame the discussion and analysis. Sometimes participants get stuck on the best theory for each situation, rather than thinking eclectically and using theories that make the most sense to them. As new professionals develop more sophisticated ways of analyzing and making sense of situations, you can focus more on that aspect of development.

Embedded within our developmental theory is leadership development theory. The social change model of leadership development (Higher Education Research Institute [HERI], 1996), the relational leadership model (Komives, Lucas, & McMahon, 2007), and the servant leadership approach (Greenleaf, 1977) all provide an approach to analyzing the cases with an emphasis on the leader's role. The leadership challenge model (Kouzes & Posner, 2006) provides a list of competencies based on extensive research related to best practices in leadership development. This growing body of literature cuts across many academic disciplines and plays an important role in understanding and facilitating the leadership development of college students.

As you explore and use this case study book, we encourage you to be creative with the presentation and analysis of the cases. Many have used cases as a tool in ongoing professional development. As we develop new professionals, we can use the cases to build on competencies to help professionals move toward the more advanced levels of each skill set. We hope that this book meets your professional development needs as we continue to explore the myriad dilemmas and issues we face in our daily work.

REFERENCES

ACPA & NASPA. (2010). *Professional competency areas for student affairs practitioners.* Retrieved from http://www.naspa.org/about/boarddocs/710/competencies. pdf

Baxter Magolda, M. B. (2001). *Making their own way: Narratives to transform higher education to promote self development.* Sterling, VA: Stylus.

Council for the Advancement of Standards in Higher Education (CAS). (2012). *CAS professional standards for higher education* (8th ed.). Washington, DC: Author.

Greenleaf, R. K. (1977). *Servant leadership.* Mahwah, NJ: Paulist.

Higher Education Research Institute (HERI). (1996). *A social change model of leadership development.* Los Angeles, CA: Higher Education Research Institute, UCLA.

Komives, S. R., Lucas, N., & McMahon, T. R. (2007). *Exploring leadership: For college students who want to make a difference.* San Francisco: Jossey-Bass.

Kouzes, J. M., & Posner, B. Z. (2006). *A leader's legacy.* San Francisco: Jossey-Bass.

Kuh, G. D., Kinzie, J., Schuh, J. H., Whitt, E. J., & Associates. (2005). *Student success in college: Creating conditions that matter.* San Francisco: Jossey-Bass.

TABLE I-1: Cases by ACPA/NASPA Competency Area

Case	Advising and Helping	Assessment, Evaluation, and Research	Equity, Diversity and Inclusion	Ethical Professional Practice	History, Philosophy, and Values	Human and Organizational Resources	Law, Policy, and Governance	Leadership	Personal Foundations	Student Learning and Development
85% Placement Rate				Basic						
A Weekly Event							Intermediate			Advanced
Academic Integrity			Intermediate							Advanced
Accepting a Position				Advanced						Advanced
Advising NPHC	Basic		Basic						Basic	Advanced
After-Work Cocktails				Advanced						Basic
Alternative Break Gone Badly										Basic
Am I a Student or a Professional?						Basic		Advanced		Basic
Annual Report at Speedy College		Basic		Advanced						Basic
Are You My Mentor or Not?						Basic		Advanced		Basic
Athletes Are Treated Differently									Basic	Intermediate

(Continues)

TABLE I-1 (CONTINUED)

Case	Advising and Helping	Assessment, Evaluation, and Research	Equity, Diversity, and Inclusion	Ethical Professional Practice	History, Philosophy, and Values	Human and Organizational Resources	Law, Policy, and Governance	Leadership	Personal Foundations	Student Learning and Development
Bearer of Bad News	Basic							Advanced		Intermediate
Beating Up the Wrong Sister	Advanced			Advanced						Intermediate
Binge Drinking on Campus							Basic			
Blindsided at Evaluation								Advanced		
Borrowing Money	Advanced									Intermediate
Boundaries				Basic				Advanced	Advanced	Intermediate
Camp Out				Basic					Basic	Intermediate
Career Services						Basic				
Caving Under Pressure	Basic			Advanced	Intermediate					
Change Is Tough								Intermediate		
Changing My Major	Basic									

Case							
Cleaning Up a Coworker's Mess					Basic		
Coincidence, Patterns, or Should We Be Alarmed?							Advanced
Community Standards							
Comparing Work Ethics			Inter-mediate				Inter-mediate
Confidential Information			Basic				
Confidentiality		Basic	Advanced				Basic
Conflicting Interests				Inter-mediate			
Crisis Management and Voice		Basic			Inter-mediate		
Cultural Conflicts	Inter-mediate	Basic	Inter-mediate				Inter-mediate
Culture Shock				Advanced		Advanced	
Dating the Boss			Basic				Basic
Did You Really Just Send That?			Basic				Basic
Didn't Pay Dues						Advanced	
Diversification of the Division	Basic						

(Continues)

TABLE I-1 (CONTINUED)

Case	Advising and Helping	Assessment, Evaluation, and Research	Equity, Diversity, and Inclusion	Ethical Professional Practice	History, Philosophy, and Values	Human and Organizational Resources	Law, Policy, and Governance	Leadership	Personal Foundations	Student Learning and Development
Do I Need to Change?				Basic						
Do Something About It							Advanced			
Do You Need Help?						Basic			Basic	
Driving Along							Intermediate			
Dual Major	Intermediate									
Eye Rolls			Basic							
Faculty Are Not Immune				Basic						
Finding Balance—I Need to Eat?						Basic			Basic	
First Week of Classes	Advanced			Advanced						
Freedom of Speech	Advanced									
Freeloading or Providing a Service?	Basic						Intermediate			

Get Me Out of This Place!				Inter-mediate						
Getting a Handle on the In-Team Fighting				Inter-mediate						
Giving Up	Inter-mediate									
GLBT Students Don't Belong Here	Basic		Advanced		Basic		Basic		Basic	
Group Cheat			Advanced	Basic						
Happy Anniversary				Inter-mediate						
Harassment			Basic							
Help Me!				Basic		Basic				
Homesick Athlete	Advanced									
How Can You Find Anything?						Inter-mediate				
Huge Transition									Basic	
Hypocrite!				Basic			Advanced		Basic	
I Can Handle It									Basic	
I Don't Agree				Inter-mediate	Advanced					

(Continues)

TABLE I-1 (CONTINUED)

Case	Advising and Helping	Assessment, Evaluation, and Research	Equity, Diversity, and Inclusion	Ethical Professional Practice	History, Philosophy, and Values	Human and Organizational Resources	Law, Policy, and Governance	Leadership	Personal Foundations	Student Learning and Development
I Need Some Direction	Intermediate					Advanced		Advanced		
I Need Space for a Personal Need							Basic			
I Really Want That Job									Advanced	
I Refuse to Donate				Advanced	Advanced					
I Was on a Personal Call				Intermediate				Basic	Basic	
I Will Wait				Basic					Intermediate	
If She Goes, I Go									Basic	
I'll Go Over Your Head	Basic									
Is an Apology Necessary?								Advanced		
Is That Car on Fire?						Basic				
Keg Party							Advanced			
Lack of Focus	Advanced									

Lacking Leadership							Basic			
Last-Minute Feedback					Basic		Basic			
Leader's Influence		Advanced		Basic	Advanced		Advanced			
Learning Outcomes at High Hill					Inter-mediate					
Let the Student Talk			Basic							
Let's Make a Deal				Inter-mediate						
Limited Applicant Pool			Inter-mediate							
Loose Lips				Advanced					Basic	
Medical Documentation										
Meeting the Requirements				Inter-mediate						
Mentoring or Avoiding?	Basic				Basic					
Minding My Own Business			Advanced	Advanced						
Misadvised Father						Inter-mediate				

(Continues)

TABLE I-1 (CONTINUED)

Case	Advising and Helping	Assessment, Evaluation, and Research	Equity, Diversity, and Inclusion	Ethical Professional Practice	History, Philosophy, and Values	Human and Organizational Resources	Law, Policy, and Governance	Leadership	Personal Foundations	Student Learning and Development
More Professional Conferences							Basic			
Multicultural Exclusions			Basic							
My First D				Basic			Basic			
My Name Is Penny									Advanced	
My Son Will Be a Judge							Advanced			
Negativity Is Contagious						Basic			Basic	
Negotiating Punishment				Intermediate			Intermediate		Advanced	
New Supervisor					Intermediate	Intermediate				
One More Won't Matter							Basic			
Ongoing Fire Alarms							Advanced	Advanced	Basic	
Outsourcing Our Halls					Basic					
Passing the Reins	Basic			Intermediate			Basic		Advanced	

Personal Space						Inter-mediate	
Pre-Med	Inter-mediate						
Publish or Perish	Inter-mediate						
Purpose of Student Affairs				Basic			
Ratting Out a Roommate	Basic						
Reading the Student Newspaper						Basic	
Research Ethics		Basic					
Responsibility			Basic		Basic		
Retracting a Statement			Inter-mediate			Inter-mediate	
Seniors Check Out	Inter-mediate						
Service-Learning and Religious Conflicts			Basic				Basic
Should I Be Offended?						Advanced	Basic

TABLE 1-1 (CONTINUED)

Case	Advising and Helping	Assessment, Evaluation, and Research	Equity, Diversity, and Inclusion	Ethical Professional Practice	History, Philosophy, and Values	Human and Organizational Resources	Law, Policy, and Governance	Leadership	Personal Foundations	Student Learning and Development
Should I Look or Not?				Basic						
Shy Student										Basic
Single in Student Affairs				Basic		Basic	Basic		Advanced	
Small Fish in a Big Pond						Basic			Basic	
Social Networking Gone Bad				Basic						
Supervising a Graduate Assistant	Advanced			Basic		Basic	Basic			
Supervising Your Supervisor				Basic		Basic		Advanced	Basic	
Take Control of the Breaks								Basic		
That E-Mail Wasn't Meant for Everyone				Basic		Basic			Intermediate	
The Aftermath	Advanced									
The Interruption										
The Newbie	Basic			Basic		Basic				
The Problem Advisee							Intermediate			

Thick as Thieves	Basic					
Thieves Among Us	Basic					Advanced
Three Couples Out of 15			Inter-mediate			
Title VI					Inter-mediate	
To Call or Not to Call				Advanced		
To Fund or Not to Fund	Basic					
To Recommend or Not to Recommend				Basic		
Too Much . . .	Basic		Basic			
Training Student Staff	Advanced					Basic
Troublesome Student	Advanced				Basic	Basic
Trusting or Lack of Attention to Detail?		Basic		Advanced		
Uncomfortable With Instructor		Basic				Basic
Underage Drinking		Basic				
Underchallenged	Inter-mediate				Inter-mediate	Basic

(Continues)

TABLE I-1 (CONTINUED)

Case	Advising and Helping	Assessment, Evaluation, and Research	Equity, Diversity, and Inclusion	Ethical Professional Practice	History, Philosophy, and Values	Human and Organizational Resources	Law, Policy and Governance	Leadership	Personal Foundations	Student Learning and Development
Unethical or Unprofessional?				Inter-mediate					Basic	
Unwanted Advances				Advanced			Advanced			
Using Your Friends for Academic Advice	Inter-mediate									
Wait-Listed				Basic						
What Can I Do?						Inter-mediate				
What Do You Do All Day?	Inter-mediate					Inter-mediate				
When to Involve the Parents				Basic			Basic		Basic	
Whole New Department						Inter-mediate				
Winter Party Gone Badly									Basic	
Working at Your Alma Mater						Basic	Inter-mediate		Advanced	
Working Hard or Hardly Working?									Basic	
You're Evaluating Me Based on What?	Inter-mediate					Basic			Basic	

TABLE I-2: Cases by Topic

Case	Academic Advising	Athletics	Employee/ Supervisor Issues	General Administration	Greek Life	Judicial Issues	Residential Life	Sexual Harassment	Student Activities
85% Placement Rate				x					x
A Weekly Event					x				x
Academic Integrity				x					x
Accepting a Position			x						x
Advising NPHC					x				x
After-Work Cocktails				x					x
Alternative Break Gone Badly									x
Am I a Student or a Professional?			x						x
Annual Report at Speedy College				x					x
Are You My Mentor or Not?			x						x
Athletes Are Treated Differently		x							x
Bearer of Bad News				x					x

(Continues)

TABLE I-2 (CONTINUED)

Case	Academic Advising	Athletics	Employee/Supervisor Issues	General Administration	Greek Life	Judicial Issues	Residential Life	Sexual Harassment	Student Activities
Beating Up the Wrong Sister					x				x
Binge Drinking on Campus							x		
Blindsided at Evaluation			x						
Borrowing Money	x								x
Boundaries							x		x
Camp Out						x			
Career Services			x	x					
Caving Under Pressure					x				
Change Is Tough			x	x					
Changing My Major	x								
Cleaning Up a Coworker's Mess	x								
Coincidence, Patterns, or Should We Be Alarmed?				x					

Community Standards			x				
Comparing Work Ethics					x		
Confidential Information							x
Confidentiality						x	
Conflicting Interests					x		
Crisis Management and Voice			x				
Cultural Conflicts	x						
Culture Shock					x		
Dating the Boss			x				
Did You Really Just Send That?			x				
Didn't Pay Dues				x			
Diversification of the Division					x		
Do I Need to Change?					x		
Do Something About It					x		

(Continues)

TABLE I-2 (CONTINUED)

Case	Academic Advising	Athletics	Employee/ Supervisor Issues	General Administration	Greek Life	Judicial Issues	Residential Life	Sexual Harassment	Student Activities
Do You Need Help?				x					
Driving Along									x
Dual Major	x								
Eye Rolls				x					
Faculty Are Not Immune				x					
Finding Balance—I Need to Eat?	x								
First Week of Classes							x		
Freedom of Speech					x				
Freeloading or Providing a Service?							x		
Get Me Out of This Place!			x						
Getting a Handle on the In-Team Fighting		x		x					
Giving Up	x								
GLBT Students Don't Belong Here			x						x

Group Cheat								
Happy Anniversary						x		
Harassment							x	
Help Me!		x						
Homesick Athlete	x		x					
How Can You Find Anything?		x	x					
Huge Transition						x		
Hypocrite!		x						
I Can Handle It		x						
I Don't Agree		x		x				
I Need Some Direction		x						
I Need Space for a Personal Need		x	x					
I Really Want That Job		x	x					
I Refuse to Donate								
I Was on a Personal Call						x		
I Will Wait	x							
If She Goes, I Go						x		

(Continues)

TABLE I-2 (CONTINUED)

Case	Academic Advising	Athletics	Employee/ Supervisor Issues	General Administration	Greek Life	Judicial Issues	Residential Life	Sexual Harassment	Student Activities
I'll Go Over Your Head				x					x
Is an Apology Necessary?				x					
Is That Car on Fire?							x		
Keg Party						x			
Lack of Focus	x								
Lacking Leadership						x			
Last-Minute Feedback			x						
Leader's Influence			x	x					
Learning Outcomes at High Hill				x					
Let the Student Talk	x								
Let's Make a Deal				x			x		
Limited Applicant Pool			x						

	1	2	3	4	5	6
Loose Lips	x					
Medical Documentation	x					
Meeting the Requirements	x					
Mentoring or Avoiding?		x				
Minding My Own Business			x			
Misadvised Father	x					
More Professional Conferences			x			
Multicultural Exclusions						x
My First D	x					
My Name Is Penny			x			
My Son Will Be a Judge				x		
Negativity Is Contagious			x			
Negotiating Punishment					x	
New Supervisor		x				
One More Won't Matter	x					

(Continues)

TABLE I-2 (CONTINUED)

Case	Academic Advising	Athletics	Employee/ Supervisor Issues	General Administration	Greek Life	Judicial Issues	Residential Life	Sexual Harassment	Student Activities
Ongoing Fire Alarm							x		
Outsourcing Our Halls							x		
Passing the Reins			x						
Personal Space			x						
Pre-Med	x								
Publish or Perish				x					
Purpose of Student Affairs				x					
Ratting Out a Roommate	x								
Reading the Student Newspaper								x	
Research Ethics	x								
Responsibility				x					
Retracting a Statement		x							
Seniors Check Out									x

Service-Learning and Religious Conflicts				x		
Should I Be Offended?				x		
Should I Look or Not?					x	
Shy Student						x
Single in Student Affairs				x		
Small Fish in a Big Pond				x		
Social Networking Gone Bad	x		x			
Supervising a Graduate Assistant		x				
Supervising Your Supervisor					x	
Take Control of the Breaks				x		
That E-mail Wasn't Meant for Everyone				x		
The Aftermath		x				
The Interruption						x

(Continues)

TABLE I-2 (CONTINUED)

Case	Academic Advising	Athletics	Employee/ Supervisor Issues	General Administration	Greek Life	Judicial Issues	Residential Life	Sexual Harassment	Student Activities
The Newbie			x						
The Problem Advisee	x								
Thick as Thieves				x					
Thieves Among Us				x					
Three Couples Out of 15			x						
Title VI				x					
To Call or Not to Call						x			
To Fund or Not to Fund			x	x					
To Recommend or Not to Recommend	x								
Too Much . . .			x						
Training Student Staff			x	x					
Troublesome Student						x			

Trusting or Lack of Attention to Detail?		x	x				x
Uncomfortable With Instructor						x	
Underage Drinking					x		
Underchallenged		x					
Unethical or Unprofessional?			x				
Unwanted Advances		x				x	
Using Your Friends for Academic Advice	x						
Wait-Listed			x				
What Can I Do?		x					
What Do You Do All Day?				x			
When to Involve the Parents					x		
Whole New Department		x					

(Continues)

TABLE I-2 (CONTINUED)

Case	Academic Advising	Athletics	Employee/ Supervisor Issues	General Administration	Greek Life	Judicial Issues	Residential Life	Sexual Harassment	Student Activities
Winter Party Gone Badly				x					
Working at Your Alma Mater				x					
Working Hard or Hardly Working?			x						
You're Evaluating Me Based on What?			x						

I

ADVISING AND HELPING

BEATING UP THE WRONG SISTER

Alicia is a second-year student. She's been your academic advisee for over a year, and during that time, you have come to develop a mentoring relationship. Alicia joined a social sorority the second semester of her first year. She served as new member president and is currently running for scholarship chair within the chapter. During her regular academic advising appointment, she shared a troubling incident that happened in the sorority over the weekend. Alicia explained, "Something happened at a party this weekend. If I tell you about it, will you promise not to tell anyone? I just need advice about what to do. We recently had a national officer visit our chapter. Some of the new initiates told her about some light hazing they experienced. When older members of the chapter found out about the disclosure, they went crazy! They freaked out. They said we might lose our charter, be kicked off campus, or be seriously punished. The worst part is that they felt betrayed by the new initiates and think they are a bunch of wimps who can't keep a secret. The senior members are on a hunt to find out which new member told the national officer about our traditions. They are cornering members and interrogating them. Well, I guess they thought they found the rat. They got drunk at a party this weekend and beat up the member who they thought tattled. It wasn't too serious, but they punched her a couple of times and told her to quit the chapter. The new initiate didn't report the incident and is planning to quit this week. The worst part is that she didn't tell the national officer; I did."

- What are the issues in this case? How do you prioritize them? Within your list of priorities, where does student safety fall? Who are the stakeholders? Who is and should be involved in this situation?

- Can you promise confidentiality? How should an advisor handle a request "not to tell anyone"? Are you obligated to report the incident?
- What are your options for addressing the situation? Consider your position and your relationship with the student.
- Would your actions be different if you were the fraternity/sorority advisor? Interfraternity Council or Pan-Hellenic advisor?

SUPERVISING A GRADUATE ASSISTANT

Ryan is an assistant director of residence life. He supervises four hall directors, including Eddie. Eddie supervises three graduate assistants (GAs), including first-year GA Nicole. Ryan doesn't want to invite Nicole back for a second year because she has exhibited limited professional growth. He believes she is immature and struggles to hold resident advisors accountable. She has a tendency to want to be liked rather than respected. After multiple discussions between Ryan and Eddie, Eddie strongly advocates for Nicole's return. He understands the professional risk he is taking by backing Nicole, but he believes that, with some strong mentoring, she can succeed professionally. Eddie sits down with Nicole and informs her of her renewed contract. He doesn't go into detail about Ryan's concerns but encourages her to work hard and do her best.

After summer break, Nicole returns as a second year GA. The week before school started, Nicole was to be available during check-in but is nowhere to be found. When Eddie confronts her, Nicole explains that another GA promised to cover for her while she ran errands. When Eddie confronted the other GA, she knew nothing about the schedule change. Later that week, Eddie is called into Ryan's office. He informs Eddie that the residence life van was taken off campus recently without permission. He knows this because he received a copy of the speeding ticket in Nicole's name. Ryan is furious and confused and wants to hold a joint meeting where he lays out all of the concerns and fires Nicole. Eddie disagrees, is concerned that this approach will blindside Nicole, and asks to meet with Nicole alone.

- Why might Eddie feel crushed? How should he handle his feelings? Should he talk with Ryan? Why or why not?

- What can Eddie learn from this situation? In hindsight, could he have done anything differently?
- Eddie felt caught between doing what he felt was right and what his supervisor asked him to do. Have you ever been in a similar situation? If so, please explain.

THE AFTERMATH

Layla was a very popular undergraduate. One night she became intoxicated and fell out of her third-floor window. Her roommate and three friends watched her fall. Two hours after arriving at the hospital, Layla died. As expected, everyone involved is extremely upset. The roommate and friends are hysterical. Layla's resident assistant (RA) is trying to comfort them, but she, too, is very emotional.

- As the hall director, how do you immediately respond to the situation?
- How do you respond within the first 24 hours?
- How do you help your residents and staff beyond 24 hours?
- How do you handle the media? What instructions do you have for the students and student staff regarding the media?
- What if Layla's RA in particular is struggling with Layla's death and blames herself for not keeping her resident safe?

FIRST WEEK OF CLASSES

During the first week of classes, your RA, Lillian, calls you to inform you that one of her residents, Claire, claims to have been sexually assaulted. You immediately go to Lillian's room, where you find Claire. She is clearly intoxicated and accuses a popular male hockey player of the assault. Claire recounts a very vivid story detailing the attack and agrees to go to the hospital. Upon arriving at the hospital, you immediately contact the dean of students. She wants to know every detail of the attack and pushes you for specific, detailed information. The next day, Claire doesn't remember anything. Claire's blood tested positive for Rohypnol, the date rape drug. Word about the assault spreads quickly, and the campus becomes divided with some believing Claire and others defending the star hockey player. Claire starts to receive threatening messages and is being harassed via social media. Wanting a strong judicial case, the dean keeps pressing for a strong story. As the hall director and first staff member on the scene, you feel pressure to work with Claire to come up with a strong, reputable account of the incident.

- What is your obligation to Claire? How do you help her through this difficult time?
- What is your obligation to the dean and the judicial process?
- What legal issues should be considered in this case?
- What ethical standards apply in this case? How do your personal values guide your action?

THIEVES AMONG US

During a crowded bookstore appreciation event, you notice two students stealing a book. Upon their exit from the bookstore, you confront them about their theft. Initially they deny it, claiming they brought the books into the bookstore. After telling them that you witnessed the theft, they begin to justify their actions—"The bookstore is overpriced. They rip off the students every semester. We're just getting even. They'll never miss the books."

- How do you handle the situation? Discuss all possible options. Who, if anyone, should be involved in the discussion?
- Does your course of action change if you know the students? What if they stole the books because they really needed them for class but couldn't afford them?
- Role-play the confrontation.

MENTORING OR AVOIDING?

After completing his second year as a hall director, JP has proven himself to be one of the most competent, talented hall directors on the staff. He motivates his staff, has a good rapport with students, and manages the day-to-day responsibilities of a hall director effectively. During JP's annual review, his supervisor, Elena, compliments him on his performance and asks him to serve as a mentor for Scott, a less effective hall director. Scott, who has been a hall director for three years, is dealing with mental health issues, including depression and mood swings. Due to his illness, Scott frequently misses work. While JP is not excited about mentoring Scott, he feels he has no choice and agrees. He knows Elena isn't good with conflict, and this is her way of dealing with the situation. In JP's first meeting with Scott, he tries to provide him with constructive feedback. Scott becomes enraged and punches the wall. JP finds himself questioning, "What have I gotten myself into?"

- What has JP gotten into? What authority does JP have over Scott? What questions or clarification should JP have sought before meeting Scott? What should Elena's role be, if any, in this mentoring relationship?
- How does JP handle the immediate situation and Scott's anger? Does it matter whether JP is a man or a woman? Does the situation change if Scott immediately calms down and apologizes for his outburst?
- Given Scott's outbreak, what should JP communicate to Elena?

YOU'RE EVALUATING ME BASED ON *WHAT*?

In a recent annual evaluation, Sydney received a "needs improvement" mark in collegiality. After Sydney inquired about the mark, her supervisor suggested that she improve in this area by going out with her coworkers after work. Her supervisor explained that Sydney is not adequately building rapport with her coworkers by not "hanging out" after hours. Sydney is initially in shock and only nods that she understands. After having time to consider the feedback, she becomes angry. At work she believes herself to be friendly and professional, and during the prior semester, the department had a professional development workshop on establishing boundaries to avoid burnout. She spends her private time with her partner and dog.

- After receiving this feedback from her supervisor, how should Sydney proceed? What are her options? What are the potential consequences of each option? Are there any ways Sydney could be more collegial without sacrificing her time with her partner?
- Do you think a supervisor can dictate how an employee spends his or her free time? Explain.
- Have you ever struggled with personal/professional boundaries? Explain.

I'LL GO OVER YOUR HEAD

Jean is a coordinator of student activities at a private, elite liberal arts institution. The students at her college are very intelligent, wealthy, and confident. Common to this generation of students, their parents have never told them *no*. This student population has no problem questioning authority or demanding exceptions to the rules. Annie is no different from her peers. As the president of her student organization, Annie went out and purchased $50 worth of event supplies. The expenditure was not part of the organization's budget, and she didn't seek organizational approval before making the purchases. Annie approaches Jean, who is also the organization's advisor, with the unapproved receipt and demands to be reimbursed. Jean knows the policy and that reimbursing something that isn't in the approved budget is against the rules. Some rules are negotiable and some are not. This is a nonnegotiable. Jean informs Annie of the policy and her inability to reimburse her. Annie becomes irate and won't take no for an answer. She threatens, "I'll go over your head."

- Role-play the conflict. How should Jean approach Annie and her hostility?
- What are Jean's options during and after the confrontation? What are the advantages and disadvantages of each option?

- What if Annie goes back to the organization and bullies its members into approving her expenditure? If you were the organization's advisor, how would you handle this conflict?

ADVISING NPHC

Abigail is hired to work with fraternities and sororities on campus overseeing the governance and leadership training of all groups, including social, service, and leadership Greek organizations. While Abigail is a member of a predominantly White social sorority and has advised similar groups, she has never advised any National Pan-Hellenic Council (NPHC) or predominantly African American fraternities and sororities. Unknown to Abigail, Duane, a member of the Multicultural Student Services Office, always advised these groups. Due to low enrollments and ineffective advising, the dean of students decided to hire Abigail as the new Greek advisor and align the advisement of all of these groups under her. Duane is not happy with the change and is extremely upset that an inexperienced White woman is assigned to oversee "his" groups. Although Abigail is the assigned advisor, Duane attends every meeting and regularly contributes to the discussion, and the students often direct their questions to Duane.

- What is the primary issue? What are Abigail's options? What are the potential outcomes of each option?
- What should be her approach to gaining the confidence and trust of the students?
- Is Abigail qualified to advise a predominantly African American student organization? Why or why not? Can she be an advocate for students of color if she is not a person of color?

SENIORS CHECK OUT

The student organization you advise has longevity in its membership. Students often join as freshmen and continue their involvement until graduation. Officers are elected for each calendar year (January to January). Juniors typically assume leadership roles and then hand them off mid-semester of their senior year. In the past two years, the organization has experienced difficulty with seniors in their final semester. They typically "check out" and become extremely apathetic and critical. They complain about experiencing the same events, activities, and parties for four years, and they question the leadership of the juniors by challenging their decisions and disrupting meetings.

- As the advisor to this group, how do you handle the situation, if at all? What are your options? Do you handle the problems? Is this a learning opportunity for the current officers?
- What if the current officers' solution is to remove the disruptive seniors from the organization? Is the attitude, "We don't need them anyway," appropriate in this situation?
- What do you think is the root of the seniors' negativity? If the organization does the same events, programs, and parties every year, do you doubt why the seniors are bored and disenfranchised with the group?

FREEDOM OF SPEECH

At State University, Theta Theta Theta fraternity is known for holding the best parties on campus. Its annual Halloween Party is famous. Students dress in outrageous costumes seeking the coveted prize for most original costume. This year, a group of brothers solicited help from a few women and all dressed in the theme of slaves and slave owners. The men dressed as plantation owners and the women were dressed in rags, chains, and blackface. Multiple pictures of the group were posted on various social media sites, and they spread like wildfire throughout campus. Most of the peer comments commended the group for their creativity; those who questioned the inappropriate costumes were chastised with comments like: "Where is your sense of humor? It's Halloween!" The VP for student affairs calls Janel, the Greek advisor, irate. He demands that Janel kick the fraternity off campus, saying that

Janel should send "a clear message that this type of racist and inappropriate behavior will not be tolerated at this university."

- How should Janel respond to her vice president? Should she consider freedom-of-speech issues?
- Can the university eliminate the fraternity based on its members' behavior? Is your response different if this happened at a private institution versus a public one?
- What role, if any, should the Interfraternity Council (IFC) play in disciplining this chapter? Review your organization's disciplinary guidelines as spelled out in the student handbook and in the IFC policies and procedures. How might this group be disciplined, given protection under the first amendment?

UNCOMFORTABLE WITH INSTRUCTOR

Dr. Jones supervises the undergraduate service-learning course, which is part of an undergraduate minor in leadership. Lea, an adjunct instructor in the program, has a good rapport with many of her students. Recently, a student, Desiree, discussed with Lea her concerns regarding Dr. Jones. Desiree relayed that many of the female students are uncomfortable with this instructor's persistent sexual references and jokes. Others resent the instructor's habit of touching them on the arm or the shoulder while at service sites.

- What are the primary and secondary problems in this case? What are Lea's options for handling the identified problems? What are the pros and cons of each approach?
- What if the student refuses to submit a written complaint? What if she refuses to allow you to use her name?
- Discuss the ethical principles, if any, that Dr. Jones has violated.
- Have you ever been in a situation when a student started the conversation with, "I need to tell you something, but before I do, you have to promise you won't tell anyone." How did you handle this?

BORROWING MONEY

As an academic advisor reviews records to prepare for academic advising, he notices one student who stands out. The individual is an older student with evident potential. Although he had exhibited high motivation when he returned to college after serving in the military, his academic record shows a pattern of low achievement, with each semester's record worse than the previous one. The advisor recalls a meeting with this student in his first year and is troubled by his subsequent lack of performance. He asks the student to come in and see him. After missing two appointments, the student eventually shows up looking disheveled and very tired. His nose constantly runs, he sniffs, and he is uncommunicative. The advising session is unsatisfactory, and the academic advisor continues to be troubled.

About three weeks later, the student approaches the advisor and says he must talk to him. He wants to borrow $500. When the advisor presses him about why he needs the money, the student confesses that he has developed a dependence on cocaine and has been purchasing it from another veteran who also supplies others on campus. He names the other student who is demanding payment and begs the advisor not to tell anyone.

- What are the key issues in this case? What assumptions might the advisor make? How might he determine the facts? What actions might he take?
- If the academic advisor promises confidentiality, can he do so and still adhere to the ethical principle of being faithful to the institution and state laws? Would the advisor violate the principle of benefiting others if he did not report to the appropriate institutional authorities the names of the student allegedly supplying cocaine? If he does take action, however, is the advisor violating the principles of being faithful and respecting the autonomy of the student?
- What legal issues should be considered in this case?

PUBLISH OR PERISH

Maureen is a candidate for a master's degree and has elected to do a thesis research project for six of her 36 semester hours. Her advisor, Professor Shady, is engaged in a long-term research project dealing with the characteristics of student athletes. While Maureen contributed little to the research design, she did invest more than a thousand hours in the project, not counting the time involved in writing the thesis itself. The results of Maureen's portion of the larger investigation seem important enough to warrant a journal article. Professor Shady indicates his willingness to write and submit the article for publication with a footnote to acknowledge Maureen's contribution.

- What is the central problem in this case? What are Maureen's options at this point?
- What if publication expectations were not discussed up front? What if Maureen wants to earn her PhD, and publication is required for admission? What if Maureen needs a glowing recommendation from Professor Shady to get into the PhD program? What if Professor Shady knows the PhD program director?
- Based on the option you deem most appropriate to resolve the problem, role-play the conversation between Maureen and Professor Shady.

LACK OF FOCUS

Eric lacks focus on a particular field or major. He works 30+ hours per week to help cover his tuition costs. He is uncertain about what majors are available and is skeptical of the advising process. His last academic advisor tried to reinforce the value of an advisement session for Eric. He reviewed Eric's major options and his general education requirements. While Eric appreciated the information, he left the advising meeting confused, overwhelmed, and frustrated. A month after his initial appointment, Eric sought out advisement from a different academic advisor—Emily. Emily noticed a decline in Eric's grade point average and that he remains undeclared.

- Should Emily see Eric or refer him back to his original advisor? Why? What if Emily already has an overwhelming advising load? What if Eric's original advisor is known for being blunt, direct, and critical of students?
- How should Emily approach the advising session? What strategies should she use to help ensure that Eric understands the advising process?

- Should Emily follow up with Eric's original advisor? How, if at all, should she approach the situation?

USING YOUR FRIENDS FOR ACADEMIC ADVICE

Carl is pursuing a double major. He does not understand the need for general education and is quick to dismiss enrolling in these classes. Although his academic advisor reinforced the need to complete his general education classes, Carl is resistant. He recently decided to rely on academic advice from his friends rather than his advisor. He trusts the "wisdom" of his friends and wants to take upper-level courses as a freshman.

- As Carl's academic advisor, what are your options for handling his advising? What are the pros and cons of each option?
- If you are frustrated and choose to stop advising Carl and focus on your other advisees, what might be the consequences for you? For Carl?
- Students can often be frustrating. How do you keep yourself motivated when working with challenging students?

PRE-MED

Helen is determined to be a doctor. She is currently a pre-med student and biology major. At your advising meeting with Helen, you notice that she has her schedule mapped out. Her schedule includes various science courses, including multiple courses that she intends to take more than once. Upon inquiring Helen tells you, "I don't do very well in my science courses. Most times I fail the first time, so I'm building the retakes into my schedule."

You clarify, "So you are a pre-med major and you struggle with the sciences? How many science courses have you already repeated?"

Helen answers, "I've retaken two so far. I have chemistry next semester, and I heard it's really hard. I might have to retake it more than once."

Stunned, you need a moment to think about how to discuss Helen's schedule with her.

- What are your options for handling this advising session?
- Should you use this opportunity to emphasize other key factors in medical school admissions? Should you discuss other career options? What are the pros and cons of this approach?
- What if in talking with Helen, you determine that medical school is her parents' dream, not hers? What if she tells you that art is her passion, but her parents see no future in art? What if she is terrified of disappointing her parents? What if they refuse to pay for college unless she is a pre-med major?

GIVING UP

You are the academic advisor for Lakeisha, an above-average, African American student from a rural area. She is the first in her family to attend college, and her parents are extremely proud of her. She attended a competitive magnet high school, earned an A average, and did very well on the SAT. She is considering pre-med and wants to be a pediatrician. When you first meet her at orientation, she is full of energy and excited about getting involved in the biology club and in the African American Student Association (AASA). She also hopes to get a work-study job in the science lab.

When Lakeisha meets with you at mid-term for her advising appointment, she slumps in her chair and does not make eye contact. She has gained a lot of weight and her clothes are rumpled. She is earning Cs and Ds in calculus and biology. Through her hesitant replies, you learn that math and science are tougher than she expected. She says she is dumber than she thought. She admits to skipping class because "it doesn't matter if I go." She stopped going to work and has lost her job. She attended a few AASA meetings but says she just doesn't have the energy to get out and meet people. She tells you she's thought about going home, but she's sure her family would just say she's a failure. She says she knows you can't help, so maybe she'll just "give up."

- As Lakeisha's advisor, what are your options? What are the problems in this case? Brainstorm possible resolutions to each problem.

- At what point, if at all, do you get her parents involved? When do they legally have a right to be informed about the mental state of their daughter?
- Role-play your conversation with Lakeisha. What are your follow-up strategies? Short term? Long term?

DUAL MAJOR

You receive an e-mail from one of your academic advisees who is attempting to combine a major in your college with a major in another college. He had filed all the paperwork to enroll in both programs, and he has your permission and permission from an advisor at the other college. He is scheduling courses on track for both degrees. He writes in distress, saying that the petitions for exceptions to degree requirements that the other college and department had approved are in jeopardy. A new department chairperson has reviewed his records and wants to rescind some of the exceptions. He has talked with the assistant to the dean in the other college, and she was not helpful. His advisor from the other college is reluctant to disagree with the new chairperson. The student feels frustrated. Until now, he believed he would be able to graduate at the end of the next semester with both majors.

- What are your options for advising the student? What key stakeholders should be involved in the discussion?
- What political implications do you need to consider?

RATTING OUT A ROOMMATE

In a casual conversation, one of your advisees, Lissette, happens to mention that her roommate, Melody, is deceiving one of her instructors into thinking she is ill so she can get extra time to complete her tests and writing assignments. Melody also cheated on her last test. Lissette refers to her roommate's instructor by name, without realizing that you know the instructor personally. Lissette also doesn't realize that she has inadvertently made you aware of an instance of academic dishonesty.

- How should you approach your conversation with Lissette? If you opt to inform the instructor, should you relay this information to Lissette? Why or why not? What if she refuses to let you tell the instructor?
- Are the things shared in an advising appointment confidential? Why or why not?

CHANGING MY MAJOR

Sally is a 20-year-old engineering student who has completed 75 credits with a 4.0 average. She recently scheduled an advising appointment with you to discuss changing her major. A successful theater performer in both her hometown and on campus, she would much rather major in theater and become an actress. You learn from Sally that her father is the sole financial provider for her education, and he has threatened to stop paying for college if she changes her major.

- How would you advise Sally?
- How would you approach the situation with her father if Sally gives you permission to talk with him?
- How would you conduct a meeting with Sally and her father?

HOMESICK ATHLETE

Kai is a transfer student from a community college where he played baseball. He transferred to a large four-year public university with a high-ranking baseball program. He was heavily recruited as a good prospect for the baseball program. He did very well at the community college and felt very much part of the college community. Two months into life at his new university, he is not feeling part of the campus or the community. The baseball team has been supportive, but he still feels new and not yet embedded in their culture. Kai begins to retreat more and more to his room. After a conversation with his mom, he decides to talk to someone at the university. He seeks out his RA and tells her he is feeling very homesick and thinking of leaving the university.

- What are the issues in this case?
- Analyze the issues from the perspective of the RA. Who would you connect Kai with? What offices would you approach to support Kai?
- Discuss and develop a strategy to work with transfer students. Does the strategy look different for athletes who are transfer students? If yes, how?

2

ASSESSMENT, EVALUATION, AND RESEARCH

LEARNING OUTCOMES AT HIGH HILL

Mona is the director of learning outcomes at High Hill University. This role is new to the division of student affairs; however, the culture of evaluation and assessment at High Hill is strong. Mona has been in the position for two years and is approaching her first national accreditation visit. As part of her job, she is responsible for submitting the outcomes data from the student affairs division.

She quickly realizes that data at High Hill are tremendously unreliable or nonexistent for many offices. The advising office recently conducted a CAS self-study, but she can find no other reliable data sources to assist her in her reporting. Mona has four weeks to submit the final report for review prior to the visit.

- If you were Mona, how would you begin addressing this issue?
- What ethical issues are involved in using data you believe are inaccurate?
- Discuss a plan for Mona as the university approaches this accreditation visit.

ANNUAL REPORT AT SPEEDY COLLEGE

Each year departments and units in student affairs at Speedy College submit reports that describe and document yearly activities and contributions to student learning. The template of what to include is standard; however, departments and units are encouraged to be creative with format and presentation. Annually, at an end-of-the-year summit, each unit presents its annual report to cabinet-level leadership.

Devan is a unit-level director and extremely creative and outgoing. Sarah is also a unit-level director but is much more reserved and introverted than Devan. At lunch two months before the summit, Sarah asks Devan his plans for his annual report and presentation at the summit. He goes through his ideas and plans, which include making a video of individuals in the unit. He also is working with marketing to create a brochure in the shape of a suitcase that he will pass out to cabinet leaders.

A week before the summit, Devan hears Rosa talking in the main office about Sarah's plans for the summit. She is going on and on about what her unit is doing and how cool it will be. Rosa works with Sarah but is good friends with Liz, who works in Devan's unit. The more Devan hears, the more it sounds like his unit plans for the summit. After Rosa leaves, Liz comes to Devan's door with a worried look on her face and asks, "How did their unit find out about our video and plans? It sounds like they have completely copied our ideas." At this point the summit is in one week.

- If you are Devan, what do you do?
- How do you approach Sarah to clarify her plans?
- If Sarah did copy Devan's idea, is that unethical?

RESEARCH ETHICS

Hannah is committed to designing research procedures to assess advising effectiveness. She is convinced that to obtain valid data, she must keep the research participants ignorant in many respects. Thus, she thinks it is important that the students she advises be unaware that they are being studied and unaware of the hypothesis under investigation. Although she agrees that some ethical issues may be raised by her failure to inform her students, she believes that good research designs call for such procedures. She does not want to influence her students and thus bias the results of her study, so she chooses to keep information from them. She contends that her practices are justified because there are no negative consequences or risks involved with her research. She further contends that if she is able to refine her advising techniques through her research efforts with her students, both they and future students will benefit.

- What are your concerns, if any, regarding Hannah's research? Discuss the pros and cons to her approach.
- What do members of the institutional review board (IRB) think of her research? Based on what you know, would her research receive IRB approval? Do the risks outweigh the benefits?
- How would you suggest, if you think you should, changing the research protocol?

3

EQUITY, DIVERSITY, AND INCLUSION

GROUP CHEAT

Rajab, a very reliable and ethical student leader, comes to you, his mentor and organizational advisor, to report a cheating ring in the college of engineering. According to Rajab, there is a group of six Middle Eastern students who cheat on every exam. They text each other and use signals to share answers, and recently accessed a faculty member's computer to steal exam questions. Most of the students know it is happening, but no one has come forward. Rajab tried to confront the ringleader but he responded by declaring, "It's part of our culture to help each other and share information. I would think you would understand better than anyone." Rajab is very upset because these students outperform him on every exam.

- What are your options for advising Rajab? Role-play the best option.
- As an employee of the university, are you legally obligated to report the accusation? Are you ethically obligated?
- What if Rajab feels threatened by the cheaters? What would you do if he refuses to turn them in because he fears retaliation?
- What role does the students' cultural background play in this case? Explain.

MINDING MY OWN BUSINESS

Margie, an administrator of the university and a member of the leadership awards committee, is commuting between campuses on the university bus. Two students, whom she doesn't recognize, are sitting in front of her discussing the upcoming leadership awards banquet. The banquet is an annual event where student leaders are recognized and prestigious awards are given for outstanding leadership contributions during the academic year. Margie overhears the students discussing the allocation of awards. One student commented, "I know I won't be recognized because the selection committee has to make sure it has a 'diverse' pool of winners. It really doesn't matter how involved you are or the quality of your contributions; the committee will give the top awards to minority students." The second student agrees, and the two continue to discuss their perception of reverse discrimination as it relates to the leadership awards.

- What are Margie's options? What are the potential consequences of each option? If Margie chooses to confront the students, how might she do so in an educational, teachable-moment way? Role-play.
- Would her actions be any different if she knew the students?
- What if the students' applications come before her at the selection committee meeting? Should she share the conversation she overheard with the committee?

GLBT STUDENTS DON'T BELONG HERE

Javier is a biracial, gay new professional who identifies as Cuban, though everyone on campus assumes he is African American. During his first year on campus, he is asked to advise the African American Student Alliance (AASA). While he is willing to do so, his passion is to work with gay, lesbian, bisexual, and transgender (GLBT) students. The college has very conservative views about homosexuality and does not recognize a related student organization. The dean of students will allow Javier to advise one cultural organization but will not allow him to organize the GLBT students. Javier, following his heart, organizes an unofficial GLBT student organization. He breaks the rules and advocates that the students organize to be officially recognized on campus.

- What is the problem in this case? Discuss how Javier approached the problem. What are the potential outcomes for the students? For Javier?
- How might Javier have handled the situation differently?
- Have you ever been in a situation when your values did not align with the values of the institution? How did you handle that situation? Is it reasonable to believe that the institutional values will change? If so, are you willing to be part of that change, even it means you may lose your job?

CULTURAL CONFLICTS

Nasim is the president of the Saudi Arabian Student Organization, which has been a registered group of the university for the past five years. Recently a group of first-year men joined the organization. They are not comfortable with a woman advising the group, or with women holding office within the organization. Their upbringing dictated that they wouldn't go to a woman for advice, nor would they follow her instruction. The men have met with Nasim on multiple occasions to discuss their issues. Since their issues remain unresolved, the group wants to branch off and start a new student organization. This group of men seeking information about how to establish a new student organization approaches Raul, the director of student organizations.

- What is the primary problem in this case? How does the proposed organization differ, if it all, from a fraternity?
- What are Raul's options? How are new student organizations approved on your campus? Would this organization be approved? Why or why not?
- While you might disagree with the role women play within this culture, what responsibility, if any, do student affairs educators have in broadening the students' perspectives?

EYE ROLLS

Mia is a new young, enthusiastic professional who wants to change the world. She is full of ideas and cannot wait to share them, and she often expresses her thoughts without really thinking. Quickly learning this about her, her coworkers begin to discredit her opinions and find little value in her input. When she speaks, many roll their eyes and quickly dismiss her suggestions, and she is often the butt of jokes among her peers.

- Discuss the various issues in this case from Mia's perspective and from her coworkers. Rather than being passive-aggressive, how might her coworkers better handle their frustrations with Mia?
- If you were Mia's supervisor, what advice would you have for her? Role-play the conversation.
- As a new professional, what lessons do you learn from this scenario? How do you find the right balance between sharing your ideas and eagerness to contribute and listening? What are your insights about collegiality and working with challenging people?

TITLE VI

Your financial aid department awards 25 full-ride scholarships to students who are ethnic minorities. Awards are based on GPA, leadership experience, SAT scores, and ethnicity.

- Consider Title VI: Can the university award these scholarships as they are currently written? Why or why not?
- Is there any alternative/legal way to provide funding for these students?
- What is your opinion of offering 25 full-ride scholarships to ethnic minorities? Discuss the pros and cons of this scholarship.

ACADEMIC INTEGRITY

Marcel, a student affairs professional, teaches an undergraduate introduction to leadership theory course. Marcel runs all his students' papers through plagiarism detection software. After scanning Phillip's paper, he finds that the student plagiarized more than half of his paper. Marcel calls Phillip over after class, points out the blatant plagiarism, and informs him that he will receive an F on the assignment. Marcel will notify Phillip of this in writing and forward a copy of the letter to the dean of students' office. The next day, the dean notifies Marcel that he has scheduled a meeting of Marcel, the assistant dean, Phillip, his parents, and someone from student disability services. Marcel was not informed that Phillip had a learning disability.

- What are the problems in this case? What are Marcel's options at this point? What are the potential outcomes of each option?
- What might he consider doing to prepare for the meeting?
- In hindsight, should Marcel have handled the situation differently? Discuss.
- Have students assume a role and act out the meeting.

LET THE STUDENT TALK

You are helping a new student, who is accompanied by her parents, to plan her first schedule. After meeting the family, you learn that the student's parents emigrated from Pakistan to provide a better life for their children. Her father, who is controlling and domineering, answers every question you ask the student. The student and her mother look at the floor throughout most of the advising session. When the student does express an interest in taking a Shakespeare course as part of her general education, her father replies angrily, "What the hell do you want to take a Shakespeare course for? You're not going to need that in business!" The student cringes, but agrees to substitute another course for Shakespeare.

The student isn't sure she wants to major in business, but her father insists that you give him detailed information about being accepted into a business major.

- How do you approach this delicate situation? What if acknowledging the father's behavior only makes him more difficult?
- What if custom/tradition dictates that the man in the family addresses all authority figures?
- Also, what if family tradition dictates that the child does not question her parents, that she be grateful for being allowed to attend college? Or that the father is the patriarch of the family and makes all decisions?

HARASSMENT

Sophia is the director of international student services and study abroad. Recently a subordinate, Zoey, brought a harassment complaint against a coworker. When Sophia interviewed Zoey, she described an incident where a male coworker, Javier, made an obvious pass at her. At lunch one day, attended only by the two, he remarked that he found her "very sexual." Zoey felt that the remark was completely out of line because he was married. Zoey is extremely upset and refuses to have any further contact with him. She is very angry at his continued attempts to talk to her. When Sophia spoke with Javier, he explained that he meant the remark as a compliment and has been trying to apologize. Javier is originally from Mexico and struggles with American workplace norms and mastering English.

- What are Sophia's options for handling the situation in the short and long term? How should she handle Zoey and Javier separately, and Zoey and Javier together?
- What if Javier's behavior is embedded in acceptable cultural norms? How do you respect his culture but also enforce adaptation to acceptable U.S. standards?
- Discuss how you would document the situation and follow up.

DIVERSIFICATION OF THE DIVISION

Michelle is the director of residence life and food service. Recently, she hired several individuals to join the housekeeping and food service staff. Most of them recently immigrated to the United States from Central America, Mexico, and Iraq.

The employees' acceptance of these new hires had been mostly positive until Michelle began to hear complaints about the new hires from Iraq. They are practicing their "religious convictions" in the workplace. Initially this was reported to include only meditation and prayer while on scheduled break time. Then, yesterday, one of the new hires was seen washing his feet in the employee restroom sink. A number of employees are in an uproar over this, claiming, "It's unsanitary! They can't bring these foreign practices into the workplace." To make matters worse, Michelle hears that some of the employees are filing grievances with the union. Michelle contacted the Council on American–Islamic Relations and found that "before prayer, Muslims are required to wash their face, hands, and feet with clean water. This washing is normally performed in a restroom sink or other facility that has running water."

- What are Michelle's options for handling the situation? Whom should she contact for assistance/guidance?
- What are the potential outcomes from each approach? Discuss the pros and cons of each option, and then select the best course of action.
- Role-play the conversation that Michelle should have with the employees from Iraq. With the angered employees.

LIMITED APPLICANT POOL

You are the chair of a search committee for a new director of student activities. The committee reviews 20 applications and selects three candidates for face-to-face interviews. Candidates were selected because of their experience, excellent programming record, outstanding service, and commitment to students and their development. You forward the names and résumés for your supervisor's approval. Within the hour he asks for copies of all the applicants' files. The next day your supervisor calls you into his office and asks you to reopen the search. He insists that the applicant pool lacks any ethnic diversity, and that the search committee should do a better job of soliciting applications from more minorities. Until there is a more diverse pool of applicants, he prohibits you from moving forward on the search.

- What is your initial reaction to your supervisor's request? Do you agree or disagree with him?
- How do you respond to your supervisor?
- How do you relay the request to the selection committee?
- What are some strategies for recruiting a more diverse applicant pool?

MULTICULTURAL EXCLUSIONS

Paul is an incoming freshman from a small farming community. He attended an all-White school and has had little to no interaction with persons of color. During an orientation session, you reviewed the various cultural student organizations and the role of the Office of Multiculturalism on campus. Paul openly questioned the purpose of the office. In the middle of the session, he interrupted, "I'm White. Where is my center? Why are there special organizations and offices for those people? Why do they get special services?"

- What are your options for handling Paul's outburst? What are the advantages and disadvantages to each approach? Discuss the best option.
- Role-play the confrontation.
- What if he whispered his comment to a fellow student and you overheard it? Would this change your response? Why or why not?

4

ETHICAL PROFESSIONAL PRACTICE

Miriam is the complex director of Mann Square. She oversees four residence halls and supervises 20 undergraduate resident assistants and six graduate assistants. It is the largest complex at Peabody University and the most prestigious position in residence life.

Miriam is standing at the front desk in West Hall talking on her cell phone. The assistant complex director, Ruth, a new professional and Miriam's subordinate, notices that Miriam is raising her voice as she talks. Ruth is not sure whether it is excitement or anger. Ruth continues managing the desk by sorting the mail, handing out keys, and talking to undergraduate students. About 10 minutes later, Miriam is still on the phone and standing right by the desk, but now she is practically yelling into the phone and using derogatory language. She laughs and then yells a racial epithet into the phone before hanging up. She then walks over to the desk, asks for her mail, and leaves the building. You look around and realize that at least 25 undergraduate students have heard the conversation and seem somewhat dumbfounded.

- What are the issues in this case?
- Who are the key stakeholders?
- What are Ruth's options for handling the situation? How might each option play out? Whom should she talk to?
- Select the best option and make an action plan for Ruth.

- Have you ever addressed a colleague's unprofessional behavior? What about a supervisor? How did you handle the situation? Did you ever choose not to address the behavior? Why?

UNWANTED ADVANCES

"I finally landed my first job, Mom. I'm so excited and can't wait to begin."

"I'm so proud of you, Claire—tell me all about it," requests her mom.

"I'm the assistant director of alumni relations at MAC University, and my boss is a really nice man named Don. He is fairly young for a director, but seems to have good leadership skills and I think can teach me a ton. I start next week and will call and tell you all about it."

"Sounds great! Good luck with your first week and talk to you soon," replies Claire's mom.

Three months later, Claire calls her mom in tears. "Take deep breaths and tell me what happened," says her mother.

"It's just awful, Mom. He's a pig."

"Are you referring to your boss? I thought you really liked him and were learning a lot," said Claire's mom.

"I thought it was going well, until the other day when he said I was being transferred to the branch campus as an administrative assistant. It started about two weeks after I started working for him. Don asked me out on a date. I said I didn't think that was a good idea since I just started working and was dating someone else. He seemed fine with that. About a week later, he asked me if I'd like a ride to the baseball game. It was an office event and we both had to work it. I agreed since we both had to attend. At the game he began getting a little too comfortable with me. He put his arm around my shoulder at the information table and made me feel extremely uncomfortable. I said something and he told me to get over myself. The evening ended fine enough and the next day at the office he passed me in the copy room and brushed up against me in a suggestive way. He didn't grab me but it was extremely uncomfortable. Later that same day, he told me he liked how the shirt I had on made my breasts look and I should wear shirts like that all the time.

"This went on for a couple more weeks until I finally decided this was inappropriate and he was creating an environment that wasn't good for me.

I wasn't sure what to do so I went to the department secretary in confidence and told her what was going on. The very next day Don came into my office and pulled me off a huge event and made me stuff envelopes. I was surprised because until then I had been commended for my work. I asked him why the change, and he responded that he needed someone with a bigger investment in the success of the office.

"For the next few weeks he gave me more envelope-stuffing jobs, phone calling that is usually done by student workers, and other tasks that seemed better suited for the undergraduate student workers. I finally decided I needed to say something to Don when he said I didn't need to attend a big event that I helped coordinate. When I confronted him, he claimed that I needed to examine the reasons I was in this profession and that life is not all about me. He even stated that he thought I was creating a hostile work environment by questioning every assigned task. He finally said that maybe I'd be better suited to either leave this job or take the administrative assistant job at the branch campus. I guess he gave me the choice; what should I do?"

- What are the issues in this case?
- Who are the key stakeholders?
- What are Claire's options, and how might each one play out?
- If you were Claire, what would you do next? Who should be involved?
- In hindsight, should Claire have done anything differently? Why might she have responded the way she did?

I REFUSE TO DONATE

Recently the Interfraternity and Pan-Hellenic councils adopted new recruitment policies that aligned with required national standards. Some of the changes included initiating new members within a shorter time, allowing new members to initiate based on high school grade point averages, and permitting uninitiated members to attend meetings and witness some aspects of ritual. Given the ingrained traditions of the fraternities and sororities, these changes did not go over well with current members and alumni. Over time, chapter members begrudgingly accepted the changes and proceeded with recruiting new members. They amended their practices to align with the new requirements, trained their members, and informed their alumni. You are the director of fraternity/sorority affairs, and one of your responsibilities is to visit the chapters during their recruitment events to demonstrate your support but also to ensure that the chapters are following the recruitment guidelines. In visiting one chapter, you are accosted by two alumnae who are active advisors for the chapter and are strongly opposed to the changes. As the alumnae raise their voices, you find yourself getting more upset and frustrated. One ends her hostile comments with, "If you don't reconsider and amend the new member policies, I will no longer donate to this university. Trust me, that would be a huge loss."

- What are the issues in this case? How do you prioritize the issues? Are there problems that need to be addressed immediately, in the short term, in the long term?
- Who are the stakeholders and how should they be involved, if at all, in this situation?
- What suggestions do you have for remaining professional in this encounter? Does your response change if undergraduates are observing the conversation?
- Do you inform your supervisor of the incident? Alumni relations? Why or why not? Explain.

CAMP OUT

You have known Cameron for two years. His is shy, studious, and generally a good person. You met Cameron two years ago at a judicial hearing. He drank too much and became aggressive with a fellow student. Punches were thrown, but the fight was broken up before anyone landed one. Cameron was put on probation for six months. Over the course of the past two years, you have developed a mentoring relationship with Cameron. He is an officer in the student organization you advise, and the two of you have had many conversations about his future plans. Cameron has kept his nose clean until this past weekend. He and a group of students went camping. Egged on by his friends, Cameron again consumed too much alcohol and smoked some pot. He quickly became belligerent and started to hallucinate, thinking he was Jack Bauer from the popular TV show *24*. When he tried to break into a local house, the homeowner called the police. To detain Cameron, the police had to hold him down. They notified university police, who filed an incident report. Swearing he will never drink again, Cameron comes to you and asks you to serve as a character witness at his judicial hearing.

- How do you handle the situation? What are the pros and cons of serving as a character witness?
- Role-play your conversation with Cameron.

WHEN TO INVOLVE THE PARENTS

Carla is a 17-year-old freshman. Prior to attending college, she sought help for bipolar disorder. Her doctor prescribed medication she must take at the same time twice every day. Her parents are divorced and have different opinions regarding the health of their daughter. Her dad treats her as an adult and trusts that she will medicate properly. He never really bought into her diagnosis and doesn't think she has a problem. Her mother, on the other hand, is very involved. She talks with Carla many times a day and asks about Carla's medication, stress level, and overall collegiate experience.

Carla struggled during her first semester of college. She often stayed up late and slept in. If she remembered at all, she took her medicine at different times each day. She also consumed alcohol, which can counteract her medication; attended about half her classes; and underperformed academically. While she did make friends and enjoy the social scene, she didn't feel like herself. At semester break, her mother became very upset with Carla and threatened not to let her return to school. Distraught, Carla sent a text to her RA, Laurel, claiming that she intended to hurt herself. The number is blocked so Laurel cannot call Carla or even return the text.

While RAs are instructed not to bother their supervisors over winter breaks, Laurel decided to reach out to her hall director for help. Joe takes the call because he knows Laurel respects boundaries and wouldn't call unless it was important. Joe decides to looks up Carla's address and phone number. After trying to call both her parents and receiving no answer, Joe calls the local police to have an officer go to her house. Joe receives a call from the police, who found Carla safe and in her home.

- What should Joe do next? What legal issues should he consider?
- What if Carla returns to campus next semester? How does Joe handle her return?
- What should Joe do regarding Carla's parents? What if Carla had suicidal tendencies in high school that neither of her parents disclosed to college officials?
- What parameters must Joe work within regarding Family Educational Rights and Privacy Act (FERPA) laws?

CAVING UNDER PRESSURE

The Greek judicial board suspended Alpha Beta Gamma fraternity for two years because its members were found responsible for hazing and providing alcohol to minors. The suspension means the fraternity may no longer meet, participate in Greek events, or recruit new members. Members are not allowed to wear their letters on campus, and the fraternity is no longer a registered student organization. Upset by the decision, the fraternity decided to file an appeal with the dean of students. After meeting with the fraternity, the dean overturned the judicial board's decision and put the group on probation for one year. Students are very upset and come to you, the Greek advisor, for answers. Rumor has it that the dean retracted the suspension due to pressure from influential alumni.

- How do you respond to the students? What information do you need? Does it matter that you, too, are upset with the dean for overturning the decision?
- Have you ever been in a situation where you didn't agree with the decision of another person? Of a boss? How did you handle the dilemma?
- Have you ever had to stand behind a decision, policy, or issue that you didn't believe in? How did you approach this predicament?

DID YOU REALLY JUST SEND THAT?

Fumiko and Wren have worked together for just over three years and are equal in terms of position and rank. The relationship is difficult for Fumiko because Wren is fairly reserved at unit meetings, but is quite opinionated when it comes to policy and rules. He often sends out e-mails and memos that appear to be passive aggressive and sometimes rude.

At a recent meeting to discuss homecoming plans, Wren didn't say much about the major changes that will be made to spirit week and the tailgating rules. The changes were meant to address conduct issues and drinking. Since many alumni come back for the game, the university is trying to create a more family-friendly culture.

Fumiko and Wren are at lunch one day with two other colleagues when the homecoming changes come up in conversation. Wren just sits and listens while the others discuss the changes and how to make them successful. The conversation is quite collegial and constructive regarding the new plans. Shortly after arriving back in the office, Fumiko receives an e-mail from Wren. He has copied five others in the unit, stating that he is very disappointed in the process for changing homecoming. As Fumiko is reading the e-mail she is shocked; not only is Wren factually incorrect, but the tone and language in the e-mail are just rude and inconsiderate.

- What should Fumiko do?
- Discuss Fumiko's role as a colleague of and equal in rank to Wren. What role should she play in addressing his tone and use of e-mail?
- How does Fumiko balance her working relationship with Wren and her ethical responsibility to the unit and their supervisor?

CONFIDENTIALITY

At the University of Central Lake, the office of student life has always been a gold standard for professional development and growth. Many of the new professionals hired into the office stay three to four years and move on to higher positions across the country. Much of the success of the office is a direct result of the leadership of Dr. Tan, a beloved dean of students who prides himself on his approach to mentoring and staff development.

Over the past few weeks, Donna, Brie, and Jax have noticed something different about Dr. Tan. He doesn't appear to have the passion and patience for the work anymore, and he seems distant. Lussa is very close to Dr. Tan, so Donna, Brie, and Jax decide to approach her to see whether she knows anything. Lussa tells them it could just be some personal issues or a passing phase. Donna is not convinced this is true and decides to talk to Lussa in private.

Lussa discloses that Dr. Tan is sick and has been seeking an alternative treatment, as he does not subscribe to traditional medicine. Donna is shocked; why would someone do that when modern medicine is available? Respecting Dr. Tan's wishes, she asks if they should be concerned about decisions being made at his level, and, more important, if should they be worried about his safety and that of others who come in contact with him. Lussa assures her that Dr. Tan is still capable of making sound decisions and that safety is not an issue. Lussa also tells Donna how confidential this information is and that she cannot share it with anyone.

A couple of months later, Donna gets a phone call from a colleague across campus. She says that Dr. Tan was at a meeting and acting very strange, and that she has noticed this behavior at some other committee meetings in the past few weeks. Additionally, Brie calls Donna and Jax to tell them that Dr. Tan verbally assaulted a faculty member at a senate meeting earlier in the day. Brie said everyone is talking about it, and he may be reprimanded for the comments.

- If you were Donna or Lussa, what should be your course of action?
- What ethical and legal obligations do you have to the students and other professionals at the university?
- Develop a plan of action for Donna and Lussa to take. Discuss and explore the impact on their professional career trajectory.

DO I NEED TO CHANGE?

Brianna wakes up a little late on Tuesday morning, glances at her calendar, and notices that she has no meetings that day. Since Tuesday is an office day, she is very excited, as she has tons of work to do. She throws on some jeans, a blazer, and her go-to black boots. After she arrives in her office, she rechecks her calendar and realizes she has a meeting with the dean of students and potential members of the student affairs advisory board. It is an important meeting and the culmination of many years of working with alumni and supporters across campus and the community. "You have to be kidding me," she thinks, "How did I miss that? Look at how I'm dressed. This won't work." However, she does not have time to go home and change before the meeting.

- What would you advise Brianna to do?
- Discuss the impact of professional dress. What role does and should it play in the work of student affairs professionals?

WORKING HARD OR HARDLY WORKING?

Chloe is the director of the student conduct office at Grass State University, a large public university. The office is responsible for student conduct across all facets of the university—residence life, athletics, academics, student life, and off-campus housing. The office is very busy during the fall and spring semesters and summer is reserved for program planning and cleaning up paperwork.

Chloe has been in her position for a year and a half and has received positive evaluations during that time. She reports to the dean of students, Randy. Randy is beloved on campus and works more than 60 hours most weeks. He has been at Grass State for five years and is highly respected across both student and academic affairs. Chloe is good at her job but works a 40-hour week and has made it clear that she sticks to a strict schedule of 8 a.m. to 5 p.m.

Over the last year and half, Chloe has accumulated more than 44 days of vacation. Grass State allows employees to accrue up to 44 days before employees begin losing vacation days. Chloe is at the limit and has some trips planned for the summer. Randy approved her vacation in March, as the policy states in student affairs. Although Randy has approved Chloe's vacation plans, he has not shared this information with the rest of the department. Randy is a laissez-faire leader who trusts his supervisees and rarely intervenes until a situation is brought to his attention.

Sue, the associate director, works directly for Chloe. Sue lives for her work in the student conduct office and works as much as or more than

Randy to get the work done. She often volunteers for extra work and attends many campus events outside regular work hours.

During the spring semester, the Student Life Division is mandated to conduct a self-study using standards provided by the Office of the Vice President of Student Affairs. The standards are well received around campus; however, the self-study requires a lot of data analysis and narrative writing that must be completed over the summer. Sue meets with Chloe to discuss plans to work on the self-study, and they agree to split up the work among the office.

Over the summer Chloe begins taking her vacation, as approved by Randy, and begins e-mailing more sections to Sue to complete the self-study. The summer goes on, and Sue is beginning to feel that she is doing all the work for the report and starts to get angry about the situation. She confides in a colleague who tells her she needs to talk with Randy, because he would not tolerate this. Sue decides to wait as they have a meeting with Randy to discuss the final report in a week.

At the final self-study meeting, Randy is very complimentary about the hard work that is clearly evident in the report. He goes on about all the details and use of the data. As they are sitting there, Chloe is beaming and talks about all the hard work they put in. Sue is shocked; Chloe barely did anything to complete this report. Sue is thinking this can't be happening and hopes that Chloe will state that Sue and the others in the office did most of the work. The meeting ends, and everyone leaves thinking Chloe is a shining star!

- What should Sue do?
- If Sue decides to speak up about Chloe, explore the potential political, social, and work-related effects for Sue.
- If Sue decides to keep quiet, what kind of backlash might that have on her career as she goes forward?

TRUSTING OR LACK OF ATTENTION TO DETAIL?

Joan, associate director of health and wellness, reports to Bob, the vice president of student affairs at Sun College. Sun has been on the forefront of health and wellness initiatives across the United States. The office does a large number of programs throughout the year and focuses extra resources during exam week when students like to let loose and celebrate. The student leaders in Joan's office come to her with an idea for a dry program during exam week. The event is to be scheduled for Thursday night when most students have completed their exams, but have not left for the summer recess.

When Joan arrives to work on Friday morning, Bob, and two other individuals she does not know greet her. She quickly finds out they are the parents of Lisa, a student leader in her office. Bob begins by asking why Joan signed off on three kegs for a party held on Thursday night at a university-owned apartment. Joan is dumbfounded; she knew she didn't sign off on any party involving alcohol. As she is thinking about how her name became connected to the party, she is informed that Lisa was arrested early Friday morning, along with four other Sun students.

Bob then produces a cost center cash advance with Lisa's name on it and Joan's signature. She is stunned; it is her signature, but she often just signs the invoices because she trusts her students, especially Lisa.

- Is Joan responsible since Lisa and the other students lied to her? Why or why not?
- What should Bob do?
- Should Joan lose her job or be reprimanded? Give a rationale for either decision.

LOOSE LIPS

Beth is a full-time academic advisor to health professionals and also a part-time doctoral student in a higher education program at Hope University. Her office hires two graduate assistants who are master's candidates in the same program at Hope. Beth decides to enroll in the higher education study tour to the UK during the first two weeks of June. Also going on the trip is Lauren, one of the master's-level graduate assistants in her office.

The trip is going very well and both Beth and Lauren are learning a lot and having a blast. One free night, a number of students decide to stay out at a pub. Beth and Lauren are having a good time talking with locals and enjoying some beer. At the end of the evening Lauren sees that Beth is getting very intoxicated and begins telling Lauren about the office and, specifically, other advisors in the office. Lauren is well aware that Beth is drunk. Lauren suggests that they head back to the residence and get some rest. On the walk home, Beth tells Lauren that two of the advisors in the office, Nel and Mike, both in committed partnerships, are having an affair and Nel thinks she is pregnant with Mike's baby.

The following day Beth is at breakfast when Lauren arrives and does not say a word. Lauren is quite disturbed as she knows both Nel and Mike and has great respect for both of them.

- If you are Lauren, what do you do?
- What responsibility do you have to confront Beth and the information?
- What do you do when you arrive back in the United States and go back to work?

CONFLICTING INTERESTS

John is the coordinator of student success and tutoring at Barkles University. The center is the largest functional area in student affairs, with 10 academic liaisons reporting directly to John, and approximately 100 undergraduate and graduate tutors. A local charity asks John to raise money for Alzheimer's disease. He agrees, since his mother is suffering from the disease. To help, John decides to send a note to all of the academic liaisons and tutors. John raised $3,400 for the charity and is thrilled. Two weeks later John's boss, the dean of students, called him to his office to discuss the fund-raising and the use of the university property for personal fund-raising.

- What are the main issues in this case?
- Explore the ethical issues of asking people who report directly to you to donate to a personal charity.
- Is there a conflict of interest in this case?

TO FUND OR NOT TO FUND

Leslie is a new director of the Vans Center for Leadership Development at a small, private, religiously affiliated college. The center, which is five years old and offers multiple programs for leadership development, is funded half by the general fund and half by grant money. A women's studies faculty member who has received a $300,000 grant for research on HIV/AIDS education and prevention approaches Leslie about a possible collaboration. The faculty member's research has largely focused on the development of HIV/AIDS education programs for women in poor urban centers. The college is located in an urban center; however, the student body consists largely of White, wealthy international students.

The faculty member wants to work with Leslie to create some leadership programs for HIV/AIDS education. The women's studies department is willing to fund 10 graduate assistants to work with program development, but the graduate assistants will work in the Vans Center. The GAs would be a huge contribution to the center and the work Leslie is doing. Over the next six months, Leslie and the faculty member develop a working plan to present to the provost and VP of student affairs.

The grant is fully funded, and the faculty member not only writes in the 10 students for the center, but also gives the Vans Center 15% of the funds for further program development and support. The extra funding is very helpful to Leslie's bottom line and she is thrilled. When the proposal is completed, it is immediately rejected by the vice president for student affairs but approved by the provost. Leslie is confused and is not sure what to do. How can she move forward with a program that her direct supervisor does not support but the provost does? The decision is left up to Leslie and the Vans Center staff.

- If you were Leslie, what would you do?
- Explore the role of race and the stigma of HIV/AIDS in this case.
- Develop an action plan for Leslie and the Vans Center moving forward.

UNETHICAL OR UNPROFESSIONAL?

Beth is the associate director of career services at Checkmate College, a mid-size, private school with over 12,000 students. The career services office is located in the administration building, which houses administrative, student affairs, and executive-level offices for the college. This is Beth's first job out of her graduate program, and she could not be more thrilled. She is also the first new professional the college has hired in more than five years. Professionals tend to stay for a long time because of the opportunities and family feel of the campus.

The applicant pool for the position was huge (72), and Beth was not the first choice of Gia, Beth's direct supervisor, the director of career services. Gia felt it important to be true to the search process and go with the recommended candidate, but she had an uneasy feeling about Beth that she could not identify. In any case, she hired Beth after her references came back solid and her program preparation faculty had nice things to say about her classroom performance.

The first two months of work were really good. Beth was making great contacts, connecting with students, developing visionary programs for multiple populations on campus, and seemed to be a pleasure to work with. Just when Gia was beginning to think her instincts were off, she was having dinner at a local sports bar when she saw Beth at the bar with some friends. She decided to go over and say hello. When she approached Beth, she heard her talking and was embarrassed by her language and how drunk she appeared to be. Beth was telling a story and every other word out of her mouth was a swear word. Gia turned and went back to her table without talking to Beth.

Gia chalked it up to youth and decided not to say anything. After all, Beth is over 21 and as far as she could tell, her friends accepted her vulgar language. A month later was homecoming weekend on campus. The career services office always collaborates with alumni relations and hosts a tent. It's a big deal; they have food, giveaways, and the opportunity to connect with alumni and donors from around the world. At the department meeting leading up to homecoming, Gia went over the details and everyone's responsibilities. They only needed to work the tent before the game, and then they could go to the game and enjoy other homecoming events.

The morning of homecoming the staff arrived an hour before tailgating to help set up, and Gia noticed Beth wasn't there. She sent her a text to ask if she was planning to help set up the tent. Beth sent one back that she had overslept and was on her way. When Beth arrived she appeared disheveled and a bit of a mess. She also smelled of stale alcohol. Gia pulled her aside and asked if she would like to go home and just take the day off. Beth said no, she would pull it together. She seemed fine during the tailgating and even helped clean up a bit before the game started.

At half-time, Gia decided to put away the rest of the tent. She was walking to the tent and heard a group of students partying. She ignored them until she heard a familiar voice, Beth's. Beth was telling a story about her boss being "super uptight and stingy about everything." She knew Beth was talking about her. It got worse as Beth started mimicking how Gia was during meetings and making fun of her clothes, office mannerisms, and just about everything she could think of. Gia was so crushed she went right to her car and went home.

Monday at work Gia was still so upset she was not sure how to approach Beth about her behavior. Beth seems to exhibit a pattern of poor decision making as a result of alcohol use and is oblivious to it.

- If you were Gia how would you approach Beth? Should she fire Beth? Why or why not?
- Think about the implications of Beth's behavior for Gia as her supervisor. Should Gia enlist support for the conversation?
- Discuss Gia's options as she moves forward with Beth. How does this affect their relationship and the others in the office?

TOO MUCH . . .

You supervise five new professionals in a student affairs division. The office is right across the hall from the university president's office and the president is a highly visible individual. You are called in to the president's office on Monday and told to implement a dress code for your office. He states he is tired of seeing thongs, midriffs, cleavage, flip-flops, advertising on clothing, and the other unprofessional dress of the professionals in the student affairs division. He says that only some of your staff members wear inappropriate clothing, so if you can get them to dress more professionally, that would be great.

- How do you begin to articulate the president's concerns to your staff?
- Do you direct your comments to the professionals the president named, or do you make this a general comment to all?
- Develop and discuss an ongoing professional development plan for the office, dress being just one of the items. What else would you include?

GETTING A HANDLE ON THE IN-TEAM FIGHTING

The athletic department hires you as a department advisor to "clean up" the poor image of athletics on campus. You role is to analyze the messages that are being communicated and modeled to teams, and to suggest how to reframe that message to be more positive.

After one week it's clear that the coaches of the two highest revenue-producing teams are unethical and belligerent with their team members and others on staff. You continue to observe, interview, and collect data for six months. At the end of the six months, you are to write up a report and submit it to the athletic director. Following the report submission, you go back to your role in the student activities office.

A week later, the athletic director calls you and tells you that you need to revise sections of this report. He says, "This will not fly. You need to tone down some of your recommendations and what you think you observed."

You are confused and tell him the charge you were given, and that you are not comfortable falsifying information just to make some people look good. Before hanging up, he says, "Well then, polish your résumé, because you'll be looking for a new job."

- What are the issues in this case?
- Discuss the role of the advisor. Why would a university set someone up in a position like this? Explore the notion that the advisor was set up to fail.
- What are the implications of going ahead with the report? What are the ethical implications of pulling the report or changing some of the content?

TO CALL OR NOT TO CALL

You, the judicial hearing officer, find Gretchen responsible for violating the alcohol policy; she was caught consuming alcohol as a minor. While this is her first offense, university policy mandates that her parents be notified of the infraction. Gretchen begs you not to inform her parents about the violation. She pleads that her dad has cancer and is out of work, and her mother is barely keeping things together. They are both making major sacrifices to put her through college. She knows that she messed up and wants to assume responsibility for her poor choices, but she doesn't want to add to their stress by disappointing them. You don't know Gretchen well, but she makes a compelling argument and you empathize with her.

- What are the problems in this case? Is one more central than another? Should you address any problems that are beyond your scope as a judicial advisor? Explain.
- What are your options for handling the present dilemma? What are the potential consequences of each course of action?
- Knowing a bit more about Gretchen's complicated home environment, how, if at all, might you continue to assist her? What services might be available to assist her during this challenging time?

TO RECOMMEND OR NOT TO RECOMMEND

A student, whom you have known for three semesters, approaches you for a letter of recommendation. He is enthusiastically pursuing a summer internship with your state senator. Although you think the student has a great deal of potential, you have some serious reservations about him. He frequently skips classes, completes projects late, and has made many ignorant comments in front of you. On the positive side, he shows great promise and seems to really want this internship. He begs you to write the recommendation because he really doesn't know whom else to ask.

- What are your options for handling the situation? If you choose to write the letter, how much do you disclose in it? What, if anything, do you say to the student? Do you share the letter with the student?
- What ethical principles should be considered? Should you share your concerns with the student? Verbally? In writing?

ACCEPTING A POSITION

Nicole completed interviews for a new and attractive position two weeks ago. The chair of the search committee called to say that she is the committee's first choice, and to offer her a substantial increment over her current salary. Excited, Nicole accepted the offer and told the chair she looked forward to receiving the written offer. Upon receipt of the written offer, Nicole informed her boss about the offer and gave her notice. Nicole's boss came back to her a few hours later with a counter-offer authorized by the college president. The counter-offer was more attractive than the offer Nicole received from the other college.

- What ethical principles should Nicole consider before making her decisions?
- What are the consequences if she takes the new job? What are the consequences if she stays in her current position and declines the offer from the new college? Does your response change if Nicole's acceptance is verbal? What if she had already signed and returned the contract?
- In hindsight, how should Nicole have handled the situation from the very beginning?

AFTER-WORK COCKTAILS

Over after-work cocktails, the dean of students is unburdening to two colleagues, the college business manager and the academic dean. His problem involves the lack of moving expenses needed to entice a cherished candidate for director of career services. The state simply provides no money for moving expenses, and there are no other sources of funds for this purpose. The academic dean suggests putting the director on salary for three weeks before she assumes her assigned duties, thus generating the needed money. The college business manager supports the academic dean's suggestion, indicating that this is how the college has handled similar matters in the past.

- What do you think about the advice of the dean's coworkers? What ethical principles should the dean consider before taking the advice?

- What are the dean's options in this case? What are the potential consequences of each option? What if the recommended practice of hiring early is unspoken? In a professional setting, would the business manager and academic dean make the same recommendation? What if the dean of students' supervisor doesn't want to "officially" sign off on this practice?
- What if the dean *really* doesn't want to lose this candidate?

HAPPY ANNIVERSARY

On the first anniversary of the suicide of a student who leaped from the ninth story of a high-rise hall, a group of students dangles a dummy from an upper floor of the same hall, and then allows it to fall to a roof below after it has attracted the attention of other students. Medical rescue personnel who are called to the scene discover the prank. The hall director and the dean of students are so incensed by the students' callous behavior that they resolve to identify and punish those responsible before the evening is over. Students living on the floor from which the dummy was dropped are called in and interviewed one by one. While no direct accusations are made, it becomes clear that three students are the likely culprits. The three are called in individually, and each is told that he or she has been reliably identified, and is given an opportunity to confess, leave the hall the next day, and be placed on probation. The students are advised that the alternative to a confession is a judicial office hearing with expulsion from the university as a probable result. They confess. The dean and hall director are fully aware that there is insufficient evidence for a judicial hearing.

- Identify the key problems in this case. What are your options for resolving the problems? Discuss the stakeholders and how each of them is affected by each option.
- Discuss the role of the dean and his potential influence over the hall director. Were any ethical principles violated?
- Discuss your overall impressions of the dean and hall director's actions? Would you have approached the situation any differently?

WAIT-LISTED

Ali is a recruiter for a prestigious private college. The acceptance rate of those who apply is 25%. Alex's parents call Ali regularly to discuss the status of their son's application, and when they find out that he's been wait-listed, they are irate. They threaten to sue because of reverse discrimination. In another desperate attempt, they call the university foundation and offer to make a sizable donation if their son is accepted.

- What recommendations do you have for Ali? Discuss how she should approach this sensitive situation with the parents. Keep in mind that the student very well might be admitted eventually. These parents might soon become official parents of one of your students, and maintaining positive parental relations is a priority of the college.
- Role-play the conversation Ali should have with the parents.

LET'S MAKE A DEAL

As the director of financial aid for a mid-size public university, you are working to improve the university's academic image by trying to recruit more high school valedictorians and top-tier students. Financial aid packages were mailed to incoming students about two weeks ago. Lacy is one of your top recruits. Lacy's mother calls to inform you that the competing school has offered Lacy more financial aid than your school. In fact, it has offered her $5,000 in grants and $300 in scholarships. Your institution offered Lacy $5,000 in scholarships, $2,000 in loans, and $1,000 in work-study. Mom wants to play *Let's Make a Deal*. She claims that your institution is her daughter's first choice and wants to know if you can do anything to offer a more competitive financial aid package.

- What are your options in this case? Does it make a difference that Lacy is a valedictorian and a top recruit?

- Role-play the discussion with Lacy's mother. What happens if you alter Lacy's package to secure her admission, and then her mother tells anyone who will listen what you did for her family? What if others start calling, demanding the same repackaging?

CONFIDENTIAL INFORMATION

Josie, a former student, has sent a letter to you. Josie left your institution after serious drug problems and personal crisis. In her letter, she requests re-enrollment information, stating that she would like to complete the degree she started 15 years ago. She explains that when she left the institution, her mother had her involuntarily committed to a mental health facility. Her ex-husband recently sued for custody of their child and won. She is now "leading a lonely existence in a distant state." The letter is incoherent and difficult to follow. You remember her well because her behavior was odd when you knew her. You are tempted not to answer.

- What are your options for handling Josie's letter? Debate the pros and cons of each option.
- Do you alter your actions if Josie's letter contains suicidal thoughts? What if she lived in the same town as the university?
- How would your obligation to Josie change if she were currently a student? What are the legal implications of your actions?

MEETING THE REQUIREMENTS

Several of your advisees have failed to meet the requirements to enter a major on time. Two of them asked you for an additional semester to finish the entrance-to-major requirements. One of these students, Jayla, who is very personable, accepts full responsibility for not having met the requirements on time. She cites immaturity and continuing laziness as the main factors.

The other student, Aurora, who is very withdrawn, doesn't acknowledge responsibility and (despite repeated encouragement on your part) doesn't want to talk to you about the issues contributing to the problem. Both students will lose financial aid and registration priority if they do not receive the requested extra semester. You have the authority to grant or deny their requests.

- Discuss the options for Jayla and Aurora. Do you intend to treat them both the same? Why or why not? What are the potential consequences of treating them the same? Treating them differently?
- If you deny one or both, what do you need to consider if there is an appeal process?
- What if Jayla is simply more charismatic and knows how to "work the system"?

SOCIAL NETWORKING GONE BAD

Celia, a paid student government officer, recently posted a six-second video on a social networking site. In this video she rants inappropriately about the presence of Black students on campus. She uses various derogatory terms and makes many racist claims. She thought the link only went to her friends. When she realized the video went beyond her immediate network, she removed the piece from the site.

- As advisor to the student government association, what are your options for handling the situation? What role should the executive board play? How should you handle Celia?
- Does the organization have a code of conduct? A procedure for probation or removal from the organization? How might this document inform your action? What if the organization doesn't have such a document? What should be included in one?
- What do you say to the campus reporter who wants a quote from the organization's advisor? What is your department policy regarding talking to members of the student newspaper? What do you say to the press beyond the university?

FACULTY ARE NOT IMMUNE

Lindsey, a valued student leader on campus, recently informed you, the assistant dean, about comments made in her economics class. Tenured professor Dr. Radcliff frequently makes racist comments in class. Lindsey explains that he discusses the academic inferiority of Latino students and the extreme accommodations made for African American students. He recently told the students, "I wish all students were as hard-working as the Asian students." He even went so far as to publicly single out one Latino student who didn't complete an assignment correctly.

- What options are available to Lindsey? What if Lindsey fears retaliation and isn't willing to put her concerns in writing or file formal charges?
- Does it make a difference that Dr. Radcliff is tenured? Why or why not? Who in academic affairs should be informed of the situation? How do you confirm, or do you need to, that what Lindsey has told you is true? To whom might this situation be referred?

GET ME OUT OF THIS PLACE!

Carlos has worked for Next College for the past year. He doesn't like his current supervisor, whom he finds condescending, lazy, and hypocritical. His coworkers are negative about the college and are all seeking new jobs. Eager to leave Next, Carlos starts looking for a new position. During a recent job interview, the interviewer asked, "I notice that you've only been in your current position for one year. Why are you looking to leave?" Carlos proceeds to share his current frustrations regarding his supervisor and the department. During his honest rant, Carlos discloses his frustrations and dissatisfaction with his supervisor.

- What do you think resulted from the interview? How do you think Carlos was perceived? What is your opinion of how Carlos answered the question? What are the pros and cons of his approach?

- What suggestions do you have for handling a similar situation?
- What if the interviewer knows Carlos's supervisor and thinks highly of him? What if Carlos is a new professional and his supervisor has an established, strong reputation in the field? Whom are people likely to believe? How might Carlos's honesty affect him professionally?

85% PLACEMENT RATE

Heather is the assistant director of career services at a small liberal arts college. One of her responsibilities is collecting data regarding postgraduation placements. She is charged with learning where at least 85% of recent graduates are employed or attending graduate school, but she is 18 people short of her goal. Despite multiple attempts, she and her student worker, Mary, are unable to connect with the last 18. Mary is becoming frustrated with the process. Heather asks her to try again to connect with the missing people and report back to her the following week. Five days later, Mary produces the missing information on the final 18. Heather is ecstatic and quickly completes the report and forwards the information to her supervisor.

A week after the report was submitted, another student worker, Marty, asks to speak with Heather. She informs Heather that Mary made up the statistics regarding the final 18 alumni. She searched social media sites and when she couldn't find the information she made things up. She wrote that some were in medical school, some were in the Peace Corps, and others were working for various corporations. Heather thanked Marty for bringing this to her attention and asked her to keep the conversation between the two of them.

- Discuss Heather's options for handling the situation. What are the advantages and disadvantages of each option?
- What if Heather's future employment is based on her achieving an 85% response rate?
- Role-play the conversation with Mary. What if she denies everything? What do you say if she wants to know how you came upon this information?

THICK AS THIEVES

Two residence hall directors are hired at the same time. During the first two months of their employment, they are "thick as thieves." They spend a great deal of time together, and they have similar goals and dedication to students. After the first two months, the two learned that while they have similar goals, how they tend to achieve them is very different. Adam is very black-and-white. He closely follows policy and expects others to adhere to the rules. Marcus, on the other hand, sees the gray in situations. He makes exceptions to policy and rules when he feels it is appropriate. He doesn't believe everyone should be treated the same and that different students have different needs. During staff meetings, their difference in approaches starts to cause tension. They often have heated debates in meetings, and each questions the way that the other handles situations. Over time, the staff is becoming divided into two factions—those who align with Marcus and those who align with Adam.

- As the assistant director of residence life and coordinator of the hall directors, what are your options for handling this situation? Are there advantages or disadvantages to each alternative?
- When does this become a supervisory issue, if at all? Should you ask Marcus and Adam to work things out among themselves? Explain.
- Role-play the conversation involving the best alternative.

5

HISTORY, PHILOSOPHY, AND VALUES

I DON'T AGREE

Jessica is a very hard worker. She has high standards for herself and others, and she is a very dualistic person—decisions are black-and-white with little room for gray. She is a newer professional who is eager to impress and to prove herself. She struggles interpersonally because of her professional intensity and drive. After completing her master's degree, she served as an adjunct faculty member in English. After three years, she decided to pursue her doctorate in higher education administration. To do so, she left her faculty position to attend graduate school full time. Sight unseen, she accepted a graduate assistant position working with a mentoring program for at-risk college students. The program targeted first-year students who were dismissed from the college after their poor academic first-semester performance. Students who appealed their dismissal decisions were placed on academic probation and assigned to Jessica's department for mentoring, tutoring, and guidance.

Someone other than Jessica was originally hired to assume this position but pulled out at the last minute. As a result, Jessica's supervisor, Cameron, hired Jessica after a brief phone interview. Cameron has served as the director of this program for the past eight years and has a very high success rate. She trusts her employees and doesn't micromanage, and she empowers her staff members to make their own decisions. She supports a welcoming, laid-back atmosphere where the students feel comfortable. She expects her staff to be approachable and to have a good rapport with the students. Initially, Jessica finds this culture invigorating. After a few weeks on the job, however, Jessica starts to observe behaviors that she doesn't appreciate; staff members arrive late to work, dress casually, and seem to spend much of their time socializing with the students. She becomes increasingly frustrated and brings this behavior to Cameron's attention. Cameron assures her that part of why her office is successful is because "students feel a connection to this office. They know the staff cares about them academically and personally. Sometimes we can learn more from students in casual conversation than in formal advising meetings. Additionally, staff members monitor their own time. Many attend evening meetings." Jessica leaves the meeting frustrated. She thinks to herself, "This is not the way to run a professional office. If I were in charge, there would be more structure. Each student would have clear semester goals and accountability measures. After all, this is their last chance and they need to take their studies seriously. I think the staff needs to be stricter with the students, not be their friends."

Over the next few weeks, Jessica tried to fit in. She attempted to engage in casual conversations but found it difficult to relate as students talked about their relationships, parties, and socializing. They rarely talked about their academics. Jessica thought this was an extreme waste of time. She found herself wondering, "If the mentors have this much time to socialize, maybe there isn't a need for so many of them. The university is undergoing budget cuts, and they probably don't even realize how inefficiently this office runs." Jessica decides to inform the dean, Cameron's supervisor, of her concerns. She schedules a meeting with Dean Jones and relays her dissatisfaction with the department, her graduate experience, and Cameron's lack of leadership.

- What are the key issues, and who are the key stakeholders in this case?
- Do you think Jessica did the right thing by informing the dean, Cameron's supervisor? Are her actions acceptable because she first discussed her concerns with her supervisor? Would it then be okay to talk with the dean? Why or why not? What are the potential consequences?
- Remember, there are two sides to every story. Who will the dean believe—the new professional who has been employed at the university for one month or the seasoned professional who has worked for him for eight years? Explain.
- Have you had an experience with someone who thinks he or she knows more than the supervisor? How was this person perceived?

CULTURE SHOCK

Ebony is hired as the dean of students at a small, prestigious, liberal arts college. The college is steeped in tradition. Upon her arrival, Ebony quickly learns that the college culture includes alcohol and drug use in the residence halls, faculty and students partying together, and student organizations using college funds to purchase kegs. The college embraces and enacts a "work hard, play hard" mentality. When Ebony asks her supervisor about the substance abuse on campus she is told, "It's no big deal. Students experiment in college."

- What are the issues with the current situation on campus? What are the legal concerns? What are the personal safety concerns? What about liability?
- What are Ebony's options? What are the pros and cons of each option?
- What implementation strategies should she use to resolve the problems? Consider what you know about organizational culture and change to inform your strategies.

OUTSOURCING OUR HALLS

Due to recent budget cuts, the college leadership is debating outsourcing residence hall management to an outside company. A similar decision was made at your last institution and, in your opinion, it was a huge mistake. Although the company claimed it would manage the buildings as residence halls—provide programming and living/learning environments and focus on student development, the proprietary company's bottom line was to make money. It oversaw the facilities and maintenance of the buildings but did not provide student services, and it hired property managers who had no background in student affairs. New initiatives were supported only if they were financially sound. Although you are a new professional and have been at the college for only two years, you have some serious reservations about outsourcing the residence hall operations.

- What are your options? Weigh the advantages and disadvantages to both.

- How does your position as a new professional affect your credibility regarding the housing decision? Will your insights matter?
- What additional information should you seek before addressing your concerns? Do you have the big picture?

PURPOSE OF STUDENT AFFAIRS

State appropriations are dwindling, university budgets are slashed, and numerous staff and administrators are laid off. In the annual presidential address, the president predicted additional cuts. Upon exiting the presidential address, you, a coordinator of student programming, overhear a faculty member questioning the need for the office of student programs. The faculty member claims, "This office, and other nonessential services, should be eliminated before any academic unit. After all, they are the 'fluff' of the university." Student programming office personnel oversee student fee allocation, the student programming board, Greek affairs, student leadership training, major programming (little siblings' weekend, parents' weekend, homecoming, and orientation), and student organization advisement.

- What are your options for handling the situation? What are the potential outcomes of each option?
- Explain the purpose and value of student affairs. Consider foundational documents and contemporary statements. How might this explanation inform your potential discussion with the faculty member?
- Discuss how student affairs supports the academic mission of the institution.
- Role-play the conversation.

6

HUMAN AND ORGANIZATIONAL RESOURCES

I NEED SOME DIRECTION

You are the coordinator of student programming at Division College. You report to the director of the student union and are primarily responsible for day-to-day programming. On your first day of work, you spend the day with your direct supervisor, who introduces you to the dean of students, facilities director, and director of residence life. They all seem friendly and have a great deal of experience. You are excited about this job and are ready to hit the ground running.

During your second week, your boss is on vacation and has left nothing for you to do. You reach out to the professionals you met on your first day but do not get much assistance from them. You understand what you are to do based on the job description, but you quickly realize that your roles overlap with those of other individuals on campus.

When your boss finally gets back, he seems too busy to spend any time helping you determine goals. You find that you have been working at Division College for six months and have done nothing to affect student programming.

- What are the issues in this case?
- Who are the stakeholders?
- What are the choices for handling the situation, and what are the potential consequences of each choice?

- Select the appropriate action. How do you recommend the coordinator proceed?
- In any position, how much initiative should one take? How much direction should one expect? Have you ever been in a position where you received little direction and had to initiate progress? How did you handle the situation?
- Who should the coordinator approach for guidance or advice? How can she get direction without going behind her supervisor's back?

UNDERCHALLENGED

Aliyah and her supervisor have a cordial working relationship but would never be friends outside of work. Aliyah confided to a colleague that she wasn't happy working for her current supervisor and felt underchallenged. Rather than address the situation, she decided to look for a new position. Over the next few months, Aliyah's supervisor left the university to join the Peace Corps and a new director was hired. Within her first week on campus, the new director pulled Aliyah into her office and said, "I know you're not happy here. I would promote you, but I know you're looking for another position."

- How should Aliyah respond? What are her options?
- What do you think Aliyah should do after the meeting?
- Have you ever confided in someone, only to have the information spread? Have you ever spread confidential information? Discuss the situations and the lessons learned.

NEW SUPERVISOR

The fall semester started with an interim dean of students. Dr. Jones continued her responsibilities as the director of the counseling center but, as interim dean of students, also oversaw student activities, leadership development, academic advising, and career services. Due to her other responsibilities and the years of experience among the student affairs staff, she did not closely manage the operations of the division. She trusted the experienced staff members to do their jobs. During this time, the staff felt empowered and valued. Morale was high as their confidence grew.

Approximately two months into the school year, Dr. Dumont was hired as the new dean of students. Dr. Dumont had a completely different management style. Rather than take time to learn about each staff member and the experiences and the culture of the division, she immediately started questioning and changing many aspects of the department. She micromanaged the staff by asking for weekly progress reports, questioning their decisions, and seeking the input of students over that of the experienced staff. At first the staff was in shock; later they became angry. Morale begins to decline as staff members feel undervalued.

- If you are a member of Dr. Dumont's staff, how do you handle the current situation? What are your options? What are the pros and cons of each option?
- What if the culture becomes toxic among the staff? Do you contribute to the toxicity? How do you function in this environment?
- If you choose to leave the organization, how will you explain your departure to future employers? When others ask what it was like working for Dr. Dumont, how will you respond? Remember, student affairs is a small profession.

THE NEWBIE

Victoria assumes a newly created position as an at-risk academic coach. Her job description includes working with students who are on academic probation or who were academically dismissed and have appealed to be reinstated. Her goal is to provide these at-risk students with the skills, information, and guidance to be academically successful. As this is a new position, Victoria is starting from scratch, with very little direction or guidance. She was hired because she is a qualified, motivated individual who could develop, implement, and assess this new initiative. Needless to say, Victoria feels overwhelmed. She recently met with her supervisor, Chad, to discuss her role. While he did provide some direction, Chad spoke more of the need for

Victoria to "produce and track results" to justify continuing the program. His pressure only adds to her anxiety and uncertainty.

Not knowing where to start, she began by researching similar programs at other schools. After acquiring some ideas, and needing assistance in developing the program, Victoria reached out to the academic advising staff. Since many of her students also have relationships with academic advisors, she thought they could collaborate. After meeting with a few advisors, she learned that they were confused by her role. The underlying tone was cold as the advisors assumed she was hired to replace them or because they were deemed ineffective. Chad oversees academic success at the institution by supervising both Victoria and the academic advisors. When Victoria approaches him with her concerns, he encourages her to move forward, be self-motivating, and get the job done.

- Identify the key issues in this case, of which there are many. Discuss the department dynamics, culture, and political landscape.
- How should Victoria proceed? How does she build a program? Prioritize her time? Build allegiances?
- Have you ever been in a situation where you had little to no guidance? How did you respond to this situation? People want to hire those with initiative who can "figure things out." Does this influence your perception of Victoria or your own situation?
- Have you ever told someone else asking you for direction that you just need them to "figure things out"? Why? Did this strategy work? Why or why not?
- Was the reaction of the academic advisors justified? Examine this scenario from their point of view.

WHAT CAN I DO?

Joy, the new assistant director of conference events, reports directly to Sylvia, director of campus programs and conference events. Joy has only been in her position for two months and came directly from a master's program in student affairs. Sylvia has been at the institution for 12 years and is well respected across campus for her leadership and developmental approach to new professionals.

Joy is working with the commencement office on plans for the upcoming commencement ceremonies that will take place the first weekend in December. The ceremonies are co-coordinated with facilities management, and Ron has been the facilities link for the last 25 years. As Joy is working through the details, she consistently calls Ron for approval on decisions about the event. In one week, Ron receives 14 phone calls from Joy. Finally, Ron picks up the phone and calls Sylvia to discuss the situation.

Sylvia tells Ron she will talk to Joy and see what's going on. Sylvia approaches Joy with Ron's concerns. Soon after the discussion begins, Joy begins crying and talking about how worried she is about making a mistake. Sylvia assures her that she just needs to follow the guidelines in the binder regarding commencement. Sylvia also lets her know that she trusts her judgment and professionalism to make decisions and that she does not need to have everything approved by Ron. If she has big questions, she should ask, but Joy needs to trust her own preparation and she will do well.

As the commencement approaches, Ron calls Sylvia again to ask why the college banners are being moved from the stage to the ceiling. He says, "We can do this, but I think folks are going to have a difficult time seeing the banners and the stage is going to look empty." Sylvia is puzzled and says she will follow up with Joy. She calls Joy and as soon as she asks about the banners, Joy bursts into tears on the phone. Joy says that she is so confused about what she can do and what she cannot do: "I thought it would look nice. You told me that I could make decisions about the event that reflect my personality. Please help me!"

- What should Joy do in this case?
- What should Sylvia do in this case?
- What kind of mentoring do you think Joy needs? How does Sylvia provide that and stay true to her developmental philosophy?

HELP ME!

Six weeks into her new position at Low College, Becca feels like her contributions are minimal. She has attended orientation and met with every contact that Ming, her supervisor, has told her to meet with, but still has no clear guidelines or description of duties. Becca is feeling as though she is being unethical in coming to work every day and doing virtually nothing.

- What should Becca do?
- Where should Becca go for guidance?
- Discuss the ethical implications for Becca and the college.

RESPONSIBILITY

Freda is the director of career services. The office has an associate director, one half-time graduate assistant, and three part-time undergraduate work-study students. You are Jim, the half-time graduate student. As part of your GA role, you need to work at least 20 hours a week. You have no problem working at least 20 hours, and many weeks you put in a lot more than that. The undergraduate students are good, but they only work 30 hours among the three of them. Freda is always in the office. You know she arrives by 6:30 a.m. every day and have not seen her leave before 8:00 p.m. She does not expect anyone else to work those hours but says she really likes her job and there is always plenty to do. Associate director Jan is a good employee, but she often works much less than the 40 hours required. From what you can see, Freda has enabled Jan to be very flexible with her time so often that lots of events go uncovered and students are starting to complain that she isn't following through with them. At a recent career fair that you were working with Jan, you told her beforehand that you needed to leave by 3:30 p.m. to get to class. She said that was fine. Jan went to lunch at 12:00 p.m. and never returned. At 3:30 p.m., when you needed to leave, she still had not returned. You packed up the table and went to class. On Monday when you got to the office Freda left a note saying she needed to see you. She began by saying that she was disappointed that you left an event early without any notice. She was upset because a laptop that was left under the table was stolen.

- Explore your options. What are the implications of sharing your impressions of Jan? What are the implications of not saying anything about Jan's behavior?
- What ethical obligations do you have to the career services office and the students at the university? Is telling Freda about Jan your responsibility? Think about the potential impact of your role as a GA.

CAREER SERVICES

You are the career services director at a small liberal arts college. Your college, which has centralized career services, has seen great success with participation from students for the past few years. However, you are getting more and more calls recently from alumni who are looking for jobs and don't have the resources to conduct a search.

You decide to direct the students to the services you currently have available; however, with the limited staff you have, your office cannot do much more for alumni. A week later you receive a call from the president, who is upset with you. He received a call from an alumnus you talked to and said your office refused to help with his job search. You tell the president that is not totally what you conveyed and that the message has been misinterpreted. The president will hear nothing; he tells you that your office needs to develop a comprehensive program for alumni job searching and you are to unveil it to the Board of Regents in a month.

- What are the issues in this case?
- Prepare a plan to present to the Board of Regents. In preparing it, explore how you will develop alumni job search capacity with your current staff. Also prepare a plan asking for more resources. What are the differences between the plans?

BINGE DRINKING ON CAMPUS

You are a residence hall director in a hall of 600 students at a very large public university. The university has had major issues with alcohol use and abuse in the past two years. You recently had four alcohol-related deaths in two years. Alumni and major donors have pulled funding, and the president has now come to the director of residence life with the edict that something is done about this problem.

The entire department has a retreat to address the issue. During this retreat it is decided that the different halls on campus have different issues related to alcohol use, and that each hall should develop a yearlong programming plan and present it at the next meeting.

Your hall is a majority of upper-division athletes. You have issues with alcohol, but they are different, since your students are of legal age to consume.

- Develop a plan to present to the rest of the division.
- Are the issues related to alcohol consumption and use different because your students are of legal age?

HUGE TRANSITION

Ellen has worked in higher education for five years. She began her career at her undergraduate college, where she spent four years working as assistant director for student activities. The position covered many areas in higher education, from residence life, where Ellen was a residence hall director, to preview and orientation, and to advising the many on-campus organizations. Ellen left her full-time position to finish her master's degree and become a graduate assistant at a large public institution.

Ellen is currently an assistant residence hall director; she works primarily with the staff of 10 resident advisors. She directly supervises two of the RAs and is responsible for advising the building's Hall Council. She also monitors and regulates the budget of the building. Ellen's resident hall houses 550 first-year students.

The transition from a small school to a big one has shown Ellen how different institutions can be, but also how similar. Politics play a major role at both institutions, and figuring out "how to play the game" is critical at her new institution. Ellen also finds that at "big" institutions, everything is "very separated," especially when comparing them to the small liberal arts college. Offices are across campus and in different buildings, and things are "a way longer walk" than having the office of residence life, Greek life, orientation, and counseling in the same suite. At her current institution, she goes for days without seeing her coworkers because they are so far away. For Ellen, this has been a difficult transition, and, honestly, she isn't "a fan."

Not only does Ellen have to cope with a transition from a small institution to a large institution, she also has had to deal with a supervisor who has never been a hall director. Ellen had a couple of years of experience as a hall director, but she didn't have a master's degree. Someone who is younger and has less experience than she does is now supervising her. The difference in experience has created tension between the two, and the RA staff can tell. The RAs also can tell who has experience in residence life, and they end up going to Ellen with many of their problems, questions, and concerns. This creates even more tension between Ellen and her supervisor. Ellen spent most of the first semester building relationships between the RAs and the hall director so there would be communication between the two parties.

Another transition Ellen has had to cope with involves multicultural programming. At the small college where she worked, the residence halls provided programming on multicultural issues, had leadership seminars on multicultural topics, and had an active ally group for gay, lesbian, bisexual, transgender, and queer students. At her large institution, the office of residence life has no direct, large-scale programming involving multiculturalism. The lack of programming for and awareness about diversity and multiculturalism is another aspect of the large institution that turns Ellen off. She hopes to bring more awareness and programming to her hall in the next few semesters.

After reflecting on the two types of institutions, Ellen has also found differences in the student population. She feels like she is less "needed by students at the large state school" than she was at the small college. She has found that the students in her residence hall seem to want to "fall through the cracks," and many of them do not care to stand out. But, she also has found that "the state school kids seem like they are more aware of themselves and are willing to go after what they want, and that they are not seeking as much help as the small school kids." To Ellen, this means that she has not gotten to know more than a handful of the students in the residence hall even though she is making an effort, especially when the RAs and Hall Council leaders are factored in.

- How should Ellen approach change in her new position?
- Should Ellen consider relocating to a different school setting?

SHOULD I LOOK OR NOT?

Ron is a graduate assistant who works for Dr. Webb. Ron often is asked to record grades for the classes that Dr. Webb teaches. Gina is a friend of Ron's, and a fellow GA for another faculty member. Gina has Dr. Webb for a class and is wondering what her grade is for the last exam. Since her class does not meet until Thursday, she calls Ron on Tuesday and asks him to look up her grade on the last exam.

- What should Ron do?
- If Ron were to look up the grade for Gina, how does this compromise his integrity as a GA?
- What are the implications for other GAs on campus?

HOW CAN YOU FIND ANYTHING?

Xania works in the Office of Student Conduct as a conduct and compliance officer. She often sees students in one-on-one meetings in her office. Xania is a bit of a pack rat and keeps documents, books, and pretty much anything she is given. Her office has become quite disorganized and difficult to navigate.

Merrick, her supervisor, is quite disturbed by the sight of the office and feels it reflects poorly on the whole division. The university does not have rules about office cleanliness, but does have to follow fire code rules established by campus public safety. Merrick has talked to Xania many times about the condition and appearance of her office, and even has gone as far as writing up a plan to clean up her office with consequences that could go into her personnel file if she does not. Xania is embarrassed by her workspace but is unsure how to go about purging some of the clutter.

After a few weeks with no changes to Xania's office space, Merrick decides to take a drastic route and calls the fire marshal to conduct an inspection of the building and office suite. Following the inspection, the marshal issues a report of compliance and lists five items to be fixed within two weeks. If the items are not rectified, the office and university will face a sizable fine.

The items are minor, with the exception of Xania's office. She must have all walkways clear and remove all piles around the window, door, and heater. Xania is devastated and feels very betrayed by Merrick and others in the office. She is not even sure where to begin cleaning and now feels that everyone in the office is out to get her.

- What are the issues in this case? Examine the issues from Merrick's perspective. Examine them from Xania's perspective. Discuss the differences.
- Discuss the approach Merrick took in calling the fire marshal. Do you feel this was a little backhanded, or did the issue finally call for drastic measures?
- Explore other avenues for resolution. What other strategies could Merrick have taken as the supervisor? How would the impact on Xania have been different?

IS THAT CAR ON FIRE?

Hannah is a first-year residential director of Candle Hall. She doesn't have to live in the hall, but if incidents occur outside of business hours, she is expected to return to campus. Hannah is also seven months pregnant with her first child, so the staff members who live on campus call after hours only when they feel it is a critical matter.

On Thursday night, Slater, one of the live-in staff members, looks out the window of his apartment into the quad and sees a fire. He isn't sure what is on fire, but knows he must check it out. It's after midnight so he's ready for bed. He dresses and heads out to find out that it is a remote control car on fire. A number of students are laughing and cheering on the driver of the model car, Darren. It is clear to Slater that many of the students involved are intoxicated, but at this point he is more concerned about the fire and damage to the campus.

Slater is able to put the fire out, and the onlookers return to their rooms. He is left with Darren and two other students who don't live in Candle Hall. The police arrive just as Darren and the other two are about to leave. Darren turns to Slater and says, "You called the police . . . very uncool! We were just having some fun." Slater ignores the statement and tells them he will notify them tomorrow about the residence life consequences.

As Hannah arrives at work on Friday, she notices a bunch of burned trees in the quad, and upon further notice, she sees that it's the senior row. Each senior residence life class donates a tree to the university the year when it graduates. The trees have all burned, and it is quite a mess. When Hannah arrives in the office, Slater is already on the computer. Hannah asks, "What happened to the trees?"

"Well, we had a fire last night. Remote control car, police came, and so on. I took care of the fire and called the police; they're handling the legal side. I'm filling out the incident reports for Darren and the other two," responded Slater.

"Why didn't you call me? I was home all night," said Hannah.

"I didn't want to bug you, and it was well after midnight," says Slater.

"Well, this is pretty serious to me. Did you see the trees? Those are the senior trees. I can't believe you didn't call me," exclaims Hannah, as she storms out of the room.

"Oh, my gosh. I thought I was doing the right thing!" says Slater to no one.

- What are the issues in this case? If you are Slater, how do you handle Hannah's response to the incident?
- Explore what this may mean for Slater and his working relationship with Hannah.
- How does Slater deal with Hannah's perception that he overstepped his bounds?

CLEANING UP A COWORKER'S MESS

You are scheduled to meet with Jasper, a student who is assigned to another advisor. In reviewing the notes in Jasper's folder, you realize that the other advisor misadvised him on several occasions, including making some inappropriate course recommendations. When Jasper shows up for his appointment, he tells you that he just discovered he has taken several courses he doesn't need for his major. As a result, he may have to attend an extra semester. In talking with Jasper, it appears that the student doesn't remember that he scheduled those classes based on the erroneous recommendations of his advisor.

- What are your options for handling Jasper's advising dilemma? How do you handle the immediate situation with Jasper?
- How do you handle, if at all, the discussion regarding misadvising with your colleague? With her supervisor?
- Role-play both conversations.

WHOLE NEW DEPARTMENT

Over the past year, the academic advising office has undergone major turnover. There is a new director and assistant director and two new academic advisors. Despite the large turnover, the new director, Elizabeth, has worked diligently to build rapport within the staff. She created new policies that benefited the students, and the overall culture of the department has become more positive and student-centered. Prior to the turnover, one academic advisor, Dionne, requested a one-year leave to work and study abroad. She returned to an entirely new department, culture, and procedures. Out of her element and uncomfortable with the changes, Dionne became disruptive and resistant to change. She commonly refers to "the way we used to do things." She gossips about other staff members and is pitting staff members against each other.

- What are Elizabeth's options for handling the situation? What are the pros and cons of each approach? Which is the best alternative?
- If terminating Dionne is Elizabeth's preference, what steps should she take? What documentation is necessary? What if her performance is good, but her attitude is passive aggressive?

THREE COUPLES OUT OF 15

Bonnie supervises a residence hall staff of 15. At the end of the first semester, three pairs of staff members are dating, which has created a divide among the staff. The six who are in couples often do things together, excluding the other nine. Bonnie needs to consider the effects of these relationships on the residence advisors' job functions and on the overall culture of her staff.

- How should Bonnie handle the situation, if at all? What are her options?
- Looking ahead to next semester, how might the three relationships affect the staff?

7

LAW, POLICY, AND GOVERNANCE

HYPOCRITE!

Joy often discusses her weekend adventures with her staff. She tells them about her social life, including her frequent consumption of alcohol. The staff love hearing her crazy stories and she loves sharing them. Recently three RAs were in violation of the alcohol policy. As the assigned judicial officer, Joy heard the case. After sanctioning them and placing them all on probation, the staff members turned on her, calling her a hypocrite.

- What is the central problem in this case? How does Joy handle the situation from this point forward?
- How might Joy have avoided this situation in the first place? What recommendation do you have for establishing boundaries with students? How much of your personal life should you share with students?
- What lesson should Joy take away from this situation? How should she, if at all, alter her behavior in the future?

CRISIS MANAGEMENT AND VOICE

You are a live-in resident director at a mid-size residential campus. The resident directors are on duty for one week a month. Monday night, when you're on duty, you respond to an attempted suicide in the hall. The student is transported to the hospital and is going to be fine. Two nights later, you have an intoxicated student transported to the hospital and need to call the parents to tell them.

The protocol for the incidents is very clear, and you follow the appropriate procedures and file the required documents. In the past, a crisis response team has come together to review incidents and make recommendations about those affected. It is an opportunity to look at first response protocol and follow-up. You have never been invited to those meetings and, in looking at the membership, you do not see anyone from residence life on the team. This concerns you, so you call the director of residence life, who tells you that he hears your concerns and will take them to the committee.

One month later, during your week on duty, you have to respond to a call about a fire on the fourth floor. When you arrive, you realize that students have a hibachi grill and that an ember had landed on the carpet in the hall. The fire is contained quickly and damage is minimal. The following morning you fill out the incident report and file it appropriately. Later that day you are called to the director's office where you are reprimanded for not following proper procedure. You were supposed to pull the fire alarm, evacuate the building, and wait for clearance from fire officials. You say that it was a very small fire, easily contained, and you didn't see any reason to evacuate, given the nature of the fire. Since you did not follow proper procedure, you are reprimanded, and your file will reflect a disciplinary action against you. You are livid and do not understand. You talk to your supervisor about this being unfair and, if you had a voice in the processing of crisis events, you could explain your course of action.

- If you were the resident director, how would you handle this?
- What course of action does the resident director have in this case?
- Discuss the bigger issue of voice and representation of those involved on this campus. What are those implications?

FREELOADING OR PROVIDING A SERVICE?

Nelson is the resident director of a large coeducational hall at French Community College. The college resident halls are currently at capacity with a waiting list of students needing housing. Brian is a resident in the hall, a very good student, and an athlete at French. He is a second-year student and lives more than 200 miles from campus. Brian also has a single room, which is rare, but he does pay extra for it.

Student dynamics play an important role in halls. Donna knocks on Nelson's door and says she thinks Roger is living with Brian. Roger is another student at French, and Nelson is pretty sure he lives in a neighboring state. As Donna walks away, Nelson is not sure what to do with this information; should he confront Brian, watch his room for activity, or check to see if Roger is coming and going freely? The biggest issue to Nelson is that French has zero tolerance for squatters in the residence halls. If Roger is living with Brian illegally, then Brian would be asked to leave the hall and both Roger and Brian would be suspended from French. The policy is very explicit.

It may be difficult to prove that Brian and Roger are breaking the policy. Nelson decides to watch the room for a week to gather some information. The hall does not have access cards yet, nor does it require students or guests to check in and out, so Nelson actually has to watch the room door. Over the week he sees Roger come and go a bit, but nothing that seems out of the ordinary. He finally stops Brian and asks him where Roger is living, suspecting that commuting is not an option. Brian seems a bit off guard and stumbles over the response, "He lives a couple of blocks away in an apartment but hangs out in my room a lot." Nelson is not satisfied with the response; however, he is unsure what to do with the situation.

- If you were Nelson, how would you proceed?
- What are the implications if Nelson does nothing?
- Nelson knows housing is a premium at French; what are his ethical responsibilities to the institution?

ONE MORE WON'T MATTER

Beth is an academic advisor for student athletes. The course enrollment caps are always very low at Gene College, and departments often will override the limits to accommodate more students. Beth is working with Luke, who is a student athlete and needs to take a Spanish class to stay eligible in the spring. They go to register him and notice the course is full. Beth calls Sam in the Spanish department who gives Beth permission to override Luke into the course.

Later that same day, Beth is working with Johanna, another student athlete, who needs one more course for spring. They discuss multiple options, and finally Johanna says she could take a Spanish class, which works in her schedule. Beth tries to call Sam again, but he appears to be gone for the day. Since Sam allowed her to override Luke earlier, Beth is pretty sure one more student would not be a huge deal. She overrides Johanna into the Spanish class.

A few days later Sam calls, clearly upset. He states that the Spanish class he said she could overload with one more student is now overloaded by 10. The course cap was 20 and now they have 30. Sam starts telling Beth how disappointed he is that he allowed her one additional student, not nine more. He tells her that he is not going to be able to trust her anymore, and if she has any more athletes who need course overrides, Beth can no longer just process them. The students will need to walk across campus and wait to get an override. "Additionally, I am dropping all students from this course who did not have permission. You can figure out the eligibility implications for your students."

Beth is very upset and tries to tell Sam that she only put one more student in addition to Luke, but he doesn't hear her before he abruptly hangs up the phone.

- What are the issues of the case? How should Beth respond, knowing that Sam and the Spanish department feel she violated their trust?
- What are the immediate issues Beth should worry about? What secondary issues should Beth then address?
- Develop a damage control plan for Beth as she begins to address the decision she made to override the class. What are the issues for her students, especially Johanna? What are the implications for her professionally?

I NEED SPACE FOR A PERSONAL NEED

Rhonda is the coordinator of the union at a small liberal arts college. The union is the center of campus activities as well as the central office space for student organizations. It is truly the hub of activity on campus.

Rhonda is newly back to work after a 12-week maternity leave. The transition is going well, with the exception of needing a private space to pump breast milk. She thought it would not be an issue because she has a semiprivate office, but the space is just not working. She meets with Dr. Hernandez, dean of students, to discuss the situation. He says that not much can be done; she will need to either go in the bathroom or put up a curtain in her office. Rhonda is quite irritated and sad that the institution and office she loves is unwilling to assist her.

After consulting with another colleague, she decides to seek guidance from the human resources office. The next day Dr. Hernandez comes to her office quite upset. He says, "I'm sorry you felt unsupported following our conversation about your nursing. I would appreciate your not just going around campus and telling others that you are not being supported. What do you need? Please get it to me in writing by the end of the week."

- What are the issues in this case?
- Nursing mothers are not a protected class under the Americans with Disabilities Act; however, discuss the implications of this situation for other females thinking about family planning and employment at this institution.
- What ethical obligations do the office and college have to their female employees?
- Discuss the fallout if this situation becomes public. Develop a plan for Rhonda to respond.

PERSONAL SPACE

Amelia is an office professional whose work space is set up as a walk-up counter. She has cabinets that lock and keeps all office budget and personnel information locked unless she is working on it. Eli, an advisor in the office, is often in others' personal space. He does not understand the concept, even though he has been told on numerous occasions to step back. Amelia has to leave her desk to grab a file across the office. She notices Eli leaving the office when she comes back around the corner. Later that day, Wren appears at Amelia's workstation very upset. He is accusing Amelia of telling Eli that Wren is getting a merit increase. "I thought that was a personal matter. Thanks a lot. Now Eli is very mad and telling everyone. I look like I'm getting special treatment."

- What are the issues in this case?
- Analyze the issue of office configuration and privacy. What could be done to remedy the office privacy issue? Whose responsibility is that?
- Role-play a conversation with Eli regarding privacy. Who should have that conversation?
- Create a plan to address the perceived "special treatment" of Wren in regard to merit pay.

MY SON WILL BE A JUDGE

While intoxicated, a group of five male students confronted a university police officer. Jacob punched him in the face and was promptly arrested by campus police and detained until he sobered up. The other four scattered and were not caught. A police report was filed and forwarded to the dean of students for disciplinary action. Jacob's father, an attorney and judge, calls the dean of students' office daily for an update on his son's case. As the assistant to the dean, you often answer his calls. He demands that the incident be expunged from his son's record and chalked up to a youthful indiscretion. Jacob's father argues that Jacob intends to follow in his father's footsteps and be a judge, saying, "No one will prevent him from achieving his goals." He also questions why his son is being singled out when others were involved in the incident. In talking with the father, it becomes apparent that he does not have the full story. He believes his son was provoked and unlawfully detained.

- What are the key problems in this case? What are the students' and parents' rights in the judicial process?
- When it comes time for the student's hearing, what role might his father play? Is his role any different if he serves as his son's attorney?
- What if an incident report was filed with the local police department and Jacob was also facing charges through that system? How do the on-campus judicial proceedings affect, if at all, the other legal process? Discuss.
- What can and cannot be disclosed to the father?

A WEEKLY EVENT

Jared, a new member of a fraternity (could be any club or organization), comes to you, his advisor, in confidence. Last night, he and his pledge brothers were forced to drink large volumes of alcohol in a short time. They were told that if they didn't, they would be beaten. Although Jared is underage and doesn't drink, he participated to help support his pledge class. He informs you that many of the guys were pretty sick, and that forced, excessive drinking is a weekly ritual among the fraternity.

- What does your gut tell you to do? What are your obligations to Jared, to the fraternity, and to the institution?
- What does the law tell you to do? What legal implications do you need to consider?
- How do you proceed with Jared? How do you proceed regarding the next step beyond Jared?
- What strategies should university leaders implement to protect the university from similar problems in the future?

DRIVING ALONG

Maria is an advisor for a student organization. A group of 10 students plans to attend the organization's regional conference two states away. As their advisor, Maria requests the campus van and makes all of the arrangements. Before departing, Maria has all the students sign a waiver acknowledging that they will not hold the university responsible if anything happens during the trip. Maria drives the students to the conference. Along the way, the van breaks down on the highway. The students climb out of the van to get some air while they wait for a tow truck. While goofing around too close to the highway, one student is hit by a car and injured.

- What should Maria do immediately, in the short term, and in the long term? Whom should she contact?

- What legal implications need to be considered? Does the student have a right to sue the university? Maria? What role, if any, does the signed waiver play regarding any potential legal claims?
- Students participate in excursions away from campus, and advisors typically drive. In the future, what should Maria and other campus officials learn from this incident?

MY FIRST D

You teach a 101 survey course many first-year students take in their first semester. You administer the first exam and Kanya receives a D. It's her first D *ever*! During your office hours, Kanya's mom calls to express her concern. "Kanya told me that over half the class earned a C or lower. Obviously, there must be something wrong with how you're teaching the class or assessing the students. Kanya needs to get into medical school, and a low grade in your class is simply unacceptable."

- What is the key problem in this case? What are your options for handling the situation? What is the potential consequence of each option?
- Legally, what can and can't you disclose to Kanya's mother? If you shut her down and inform her that you cannot legally discuss her daughter's grades without her daughter's permission, what's going to happen? Consider an alternative.
- What role does Kanya play in this case? How do you work with her to avoid a similar situation in the future?
- Role-play the call.

KEG PARTY

A parent calls outraged because his daughter is facing possible expulsion from the university. Between you and me, she is accused of holding a keg party in her residence hall room where 25 people attended. Campus police found and confiscated marijuana, but the student claims the marijuana isn't hers. She or one of her guests also pulled the fire alarm at 3:00 a.m. She is underage as were her guests. You are the conduct officer in charge of the case.

- What legalities should you be aware of in this case? What can and can't you tell her father?
- Should he bring his lawyer to the disciplinary hearing? If so, what is the role of the lawyer in the meeting? If the father attends the hearing, what is his role?
- What are the student's rights in the hearing?
- Role-play the hearing. If the student is found responsible, what sanctions would be imposed? Does your university have predetermined sanctions, or can you impose creative/educational sanctioning? What sanction do you recommend?

THE PROBLEM ADVISEE

It's parents' weekend. You are attending a reception where professors and advisors are encouraged to mingle with students and their parents. Your thoughts turn to George, the only "problem" advisee you have this semester. From the beginning, George, a freshman who attended an exclusive prep school, has seemed sullen and disengaged. He told you he was in college only because his parents made him come. He chose your institution because of its reputation as a party school. He has missed classes all fall, and faculty members have complained that he's been extremely rude the few times he's actually shown up. He doesn't respond to your e-mails and phone messages when you've attempted to reach out and talk with him.

You've heard through the student grapevine that George is in serious trouble for underage drinking and noise violations in the residence hall. It's only a matter of time before he either flunks out or is kicked out of school. In a meeting earlier in the semester, George said resentfully that his parents are not interested in him. He feels they just shipped him away for high school and college. At least you won't have to deal with George or his parents today.

Just as that thought crosses your mind, an extremely elegant woman approaches. After glancing at your name tag, she says, "I'm George's mother, and I'm so glad to meet you. George has told me how helpful you've been this semester. He just loves the courses you've helped him pick. He says you're always available for encouragement and advice. I know George was a bit of a disappointment in prep school, but he tells me he's working hard at his studies now. You are a great part of his academic success. I'd really like to know how you feel he's progressing."

- What are your options for addressing George's mother? What are the potential consequences of your responses?
- What FERPA (Family Educational Rights and Privacy Act) issues should you consider? What are you legally allowed to disclose to her?
- What about including George in the conversation? What if George continues to lie to his mother in front of you? Do you recommend addressing the situation now or later? Why?
- Role-play the confrontation.

MISADVISED FATHER

You receive a phone call from an irate parent who claims that you misadvised his daughter, Amy, by scheduling her for a calculus course that she had already transferred from another school. The university doesn't permit duplication of course credit, so the registrar is dropping the calculus course from Amy's current schedule. This change makes her a part-time student and will affect her financial aid and health insurance. Amy's father claims he is considering a lawsuit. You ask if you can call him back after checking Amy's records.

When you read the advising notes from previous appointments, you find that you specifically asked Amy if she had any advanced placement or transfer credits, and she said that she didn't. You also noted that calculus is required in computer science, a major that Amy is seriously considering because of family pressure. You know she has no interest in computer science. You also discover that, on her own, Amy has dropped her introductory computer science class, which she also needs for the computer science major. If she hadn't dropped the computer science course, she would have remained full time, even if her calculus course was canceled. Since Amy is protected by confidentiality rights, you realize you can't discuss any of this with her father.

- What do you say when you call Amy's father back?
- How do you defend your reputation, satisfy a parent's need to know, and protect a student's rights without making the parental dynamic worse?
- Role-play the conversation with Amy's father.

READING THE STUDENT NEWSPAPER

You open the student newspaper and are shocked to find that Alex, one of your advisees, has written a letter accusing you of making inappropriate sexual comments and advances in recent advising appointments. You know these accusations are false and suspect that the letter was written in retaliation for not granting Alex the academic exception he asked for. You also know that Alex has had some emotional problems that might have contributed to the situation.

- Discuss options for handling Alex. Who needs to be involved in your preferred option?
- Discuss options for protecting your professional reputation. Who needs to be part of the preferred plan? What legal implications need to be considered?
- Devise an action plan for addressing the situation immediately, within the next few days, and over the next week.

UNDERAGE DRINKING

Clyde is the residence director (RD) of Adams Hall. Amir, an RA, invited him to his room for a party. Upon arrival, Clyde found four students consuming alcohol, but he believed all of the students were 21. Clyde is new to the area and doesn't have any friends. Amir is 22, only two years younger than Clyde.

University policy states that under no circumstances are RDs allowed to consume alcohol. Adhering to this policy, Clyde did not consume any alcohol. After about an hour of hanging out, Clyde excused himself from the party. He went straight to his office and checked the birthdates of those attending the party. Three out of four were underage.

- What are Clyde's options at this point? What are the potential outcomes of each approach? Who, if anyone, should Clyde inform about the situation?
- In hindsight, how should Clyde have handled the invitation? The party?
- What if Clyde really likes Amir and enjoyed hanging out with him?

RETRACTING A STATEMENT

Leslie is a female soccer coach at Smoker College. The program has been very successful the last five years, and the women have earned the highest grade point average on the campus for 12 consecutive semesters. Additionally, Leslie was honored in the spring with the coach of the year award. With all of this success, it comes as a huge surprise when Juan, director of residence life, calls Leslie and says they need to talk, and it would be better done in person.

Leslie meets Juan at the union coffee shop and is a bit nervous about what he has to say. Juan quickly gets to the purpose of the meeting. Apparently last night three women soccer players were seen leaving a room that was reported to smell of marijuana smoke. A resident in the same hall reported the smell, and one of the hall directors, Dana, went to investigate. When she arrived in the room, the women—all three star soccer players—were leaving, but were acting a bit strange and laughing a lot. Dana asked them what they were doing, and they blew her off and left the building.

Leslie was adamant that it was not her players and she would check with them. Juan told Leslie that the students would be written up, which would spark an investigation, and during that process the players would need to give statements.

Leslie said, "Under no uncertain terms will you talk to my players. You will come directly to me!"

Later that afternoon, Dana runs into Juan's office crying and saying that some soccer coach had called her and told her to stop lying about the women and to pull the report.

"Juan, she was so mean. She was swearing and told me she would make it so I never received a positive recommendation. I have to pull the report, Juan. I have to get into graduate school at the end of this year! She was awful; please, just pull the report. I can say it was a mistake!"

- What are the issues of this case?
- Explore options from Juan's perspective. Where does he begin to address the issues involved?
- Explore options from Dana's perspective. Where does she begin to address the issues involved?
- Discuss the role of athletics at Smoker College. How do you begin to change the culture?

8

LEADERSHIP

ONGOING FIRE ALARMS

For six consecutive evenings, one or two fire alarms are pulled in your residence hall. As the residence hall director, you are responsible for ensuring that the 15-story building is cleared each time an alarm is triggered. The alarms are pulled between 1 a.m. and 4 a.m. and always on a different floor. You and your resident advisor staff are exhausted. Since you are no closer to identifying the culprits, exhausted, you make arrangements to spend one night away from the building so you can get a good night's sleep. You are allowed a certain number of evenings away from the building each semester, and your request is completely within the policy. You inform your supervisor of your intentions, but she will not permit you to leave for the evening. She comments, "Your building is in crisis. You can't leave the problem unattended. I can't approve your request." You express your concern: "I'm exhausted and I haven't slept in six nights. I need a break and can't cope with this anymore."

She replies, "I know you're tired but we really need you right now. Your staff needs you right now."

- What are the primary issues in this case?
- Who are the stakeholders in this case, and how are they affected?
- What do you think of the supervisor's decision? Explain. If you were the supervisor, what would you do? Explore the advantages and disadvantages of each course of action.
- What should the hall director do? What are her options? What are the possible consequences of each option?

LEADER'S INFLUENCE

Part One: Cassandra Jones is the director of residence life at Chance University. Having spent the past 15 years in residence life and the past four at Chance, Cassandra is a seasoned residence life professional. During her tenure at Chance she oversaw the construction of two new residence halls, which increased capacity to 2,000 beds. Occupancy is at 98%. Cassandra supervises two assistant directors and five hall directors. The assistant directors, Joanne and Christopher, have approximately six years of professional experience in residence life, while most of the hall directors are new professionals with fewer than two years in the field.

The hall directors are unified in their dislike of Cassandra. They often complain that she pits people against one another, doesn't follow through with promises, is unapproachable, and lies. They believe the assistant directors hold the department together. The hall directors often express their dissatisfaction to the assistant directors, who remind the new professionals that while they might not approve of Cassandra's actions and decisions, they need to support her as the director. Recently, the six hall directors convened to discuss leaving the department. They invite Joanne and Christopher.

- What are the key problems of this case?
- What is the responsibility of Joanne and Christopher in this case? What if they are satisfied in their current positions and do not share the hall directors' dissatisfaction? What if they, too, are frustrated?
- What should the hall directors do? What options do they have, and what might be the outcome of each course of action? Carefully consider whom they can trust and confide in.

Part Two: The hall directors decide to write and sign a letter to the vice president of student affairs expressing their concerns. The VP interviews each member of the staff to acquire more information. Each one is honest and remains professional. They point out specific, work-related concerns and are careful not to attack the director personally. The VP thanks each staff member for his or her candor and promises that he will remedy the situation. Two weeks pass, then four, then six—nothing changes. The group appoints a spokesperson to meet with the VP to address their concerns again. The

VP explains that change takes time and that he does not like conflict. "I am dealing with this situation; you just need to trust me," the VP shares.

- What is your reaction to the VP's approach?
- What do you recommend the hall directors do if the situation doesn't improve?
- What are some of the potential politics of this situation?

SUPERVISING YOUR SUPERVISOR

Lauren and her supervisor, John, have worked well together for five years. John is more than Lauren's supervisor; he is her mentor and friend. She has learned a great deal from him and admires him as a professional. Recently John filed for divorce after learning of his partner's affair. Over the course of a semester, Lauren can tell that John's mental health is declining. She can tell that he's not in a good place and often asks him how he's feeling. His mood often dictates Lauren's day. If he is depressed and quiet, Lauren will take over and run the department. If he is positive and upbeat, Lauren will do her normal work. While Lauren is trying to cover for him, she recently made a departmental decision only to find out later that John was upset with her "overstep."

- What are the key issues in this case?
- Do you think Lauren overstepped? Why or why not?
- Does John have the right to be upset? Discuss.
- What are Lauren's options for handling these problems? Role-play each option. What are the potential consequences of each course of action?

CHANGE IS TOUGH

For the past three years, Destiny served as an activities coordinator for the student union. Five months ago, the manager of the information desk resigned. In the interim, the student manager, Colleen, oversaw the desk operations. Because the union needed a full-time staff person, Destiny's job responsibilities changed to include overseeing operations for the information desk. Undergraduates staff the union information desk, which offers a variety of services such as information dissemination, ticket sales, and room reservations. Destiny inherited a group of student workers who clashed with her immediately. She found them unresponsive to feedback and standoffish. Part of Destiny's problem was that her office was in the lower level of the building, and the information desk was on the first floor. She frequently received complaints about the unfriendly staff, who often treated customers as if they were interruptions, chatted with friends while at work, and dropped phone calls. To combat these issues, Destiny implemented new policies and standards, visited the desk as frequently as possible, and verbally disciplined the staff. Her biggest nemesis was the student manager, Colleen. She was the ringleader of the student staff and often undermined Destiny. Colleen wouldn't copy Destiny on e-mails and would take her concerns to Destiny's supervisor rather than to Destiny. Late during the spring semester, Destiny decided not to hire Colleen back as student manager. The rest of the student staff was very upset and badgered Destiny about the decision, but she refused to discuss the situation with them. Many threatened to quit and said mean things to Destiny about her management style. Destiny left meetings crying and called her boss because she didn't know if she could keep working with these students.

- What suggestions do you have for Destiny? What should she do now?
- If you were Destiny's supervisor, how would you handle the call? How would you follow up with Destiny the next day?
- If Destiny could go back and begin again, what recommendations would you have for her?
- Have you worked with challenging students? If so, explain the situation and how you handled them.

BOUNDARIES

Kiara, an area coordinator at a mid-size university in a small town, supervises eight hall directors. Since there are few young professionals in the town, many of the staff, hall directors, and area coordinators socialize outside of work. At first, Kiara tried to maintain professional boundaries with her staff, but since she didn't have any other friends in town, she began socializing regularly with them. One night, the hall directors started complaining about the director of residence life. Venting, they discussed an unpopular decision he had made recently and called into question his leadership abilities. When Kiara tried to defend the decision, and her boss, the group immediately shut her down. They teased her for being a suck-up and being the boss's "talking puppet." In her need to be accepted, Kiara sided with the hall directors and contributed to the negative conversation about her boss.

- Discuss Kiara's situation. What suggestions do you have for handling the situation and work friendships in general?
- Have you ever had difficulty with professional boundaries? Explain.
- Have you ever been in a situation where colleagues bad-mouthed a colleague? How did you handle the situation?

BLINDSIDED AT EVALUATION

Amida recently completed her first year as a new professional. She learned a great deal during her first year and received nothing but encouragement and praise from her supervisor, Jade. Amida recently had her annual performance review. While Jade offered Amida constructive, professional feedback, Amida felt completely blindsided by her performance evaluation. Jade gave her an overall score of *average* and cited multiple issues with Amida's performance. Jade apologized for not bringing up her concerns earlier but claimed that she wasn't "good with confrontation." Amida left the meeting very upset. If Jade had addressed the issue in the moment, she could have amended her behavior. Stunned, Amida feels frustrated, angry, and hurt.

- How should Amida respond, if at all? Should she react right away or wait?
- You probably agree that nothing should come as a surprise in a performance review. Why, then, do professionals often wait for annual evaluations to address behavior?
- Discuss why it is important, although difficult, to give feedback.

TRAINING STUDENT STAFF

Career Services at Jeb Community College recently underwent cutbacks. The office lost two of five career services professionals. To offset the staffing shortage, the director, Jim, decided to train three undergraduates to help advise students. Jim really believes in the program and in the development of the three students. Jackie has served as a career counselor at Jeb for three years, but after six months of the undergraduate career counselor program, she is fed up. In her opinion, the program is doing more harm than good. The undergraduates are inexperienced and underqualified and lack professionalism. Everyone but Jim recognizes that the program is failing. Despite additional training and ongoing feedback, the program remains unsuccessful. Jackie asked Jim for a staff meeting to discuss the problems. When Jim asked for input, Jackie was the only one to speak up.

- Jackie loves her job and recognizes the importance of career services. She has high expectations for herself and others. What are her options?
- What are the consequences if she does nothing? What are the consequences if Jackie continues to vocalize the problems?

TROUBLESOME STUDENT

Amir is a starting guard for the basketball team. He's received numerous alcohol violations and has been accused of sexual misconduct, but the charges were not pursued due to lack of information. He was recently ejected from the stands at the university's football game for touching women. When the team scored or made a good play, he would smack the bottoms of the surrounding female students. When campus police escorted him out of the stadium, he claimed that he was wrongfully accused because he was the only African American student present. He claimed, "Everyone is out to get me on this White campus. All you officers are racist." He called one of the African American arresting officers "White" and tried to resist arrest.

- You are the administrator on call during the incident. Campus police contact you regarding the incident to determine how to proceed.

- What are your options as the administrator on duty? Who else do you need to inform?
- What role, if any, should athletics play in the consequences of Amir's actions? Are you under any obligation to inform athletics or Amir's coaches?

BEARER OF BAD NEWS

The career center is moving from its current location to the student center so that its services for students are more centrally located. While this new location has many advantages, the center will eliminate student organization space. Knowing this will not be a popular decision among leaders of student organizations, the dean of students asks you, because you advise many of the groups, to break the news to the students. He reminds you that the students will not be happy, but that you need to make them understand his decision. He doesn't want student backlash from this decision.

- How do you feel about being asked to inform the students? Do you have a choice?
- What information do you need before telling the students? How do you break the news to them? Again, the goal is to get them to accept the change and not revolt.
- What if you personally disagree with the decision to move the career center? Does this change the way you inform the students?

DIDN'T PAY DUES

Officers of Alpha Alpha Alpha fraternity grapple with holding brothers accountable. The fraternity is struggling financially, and many members are late paying their semester dues. Three students haven't paid their dues in over two years, but the treasurer and president allow them to continue as members. Despite multiple bills and numerous conversations with the three delinquent brothers, their bills remain unpaid. They have multiple excuses for why they can't pay. They often appeal to the "importance of brotherhood" and supporting each other through "thick and thin." The organization is not financially solvent and needs the dues from all members. As the Greek advisor, you approach the president, Aiden, with your concerns. Aiden becomes very defensive and threatens to resign and deactivate if these three are removed from the brotherhood.

- Role-play the conversation with Aiden. How would you approach the situation?
- What information or data do you need?
- How much do you allow students to govern their organizations before stepping in? How do you offer suggestions/input without taking over?

LAST-MINUTE FEEDBACK

Jonas is a new coordinator of student activities at Brick University. He has been in this role for six months and was hired because he has a bachelor's degree in building construction management and a master's degree in student affairs. He was a very active undergraduate student and attended Brick for his master's degree, during which time he was also active in graduate school governance. His combined experiences and enthusiasm helped him earn his current position. Additionally, he took the job because one of his first roles is to oversee renovation of the student union. He is working closely with multiple offices across campus, and his direct supervisor, Stella, has given Jonas her blessing to use his undergraduate degree and student affairs knowledge to help envision a dynamic new union.

As plans are developed and revised, a capital layout committee reviews the plans and provides feedback. Stella is an active member of that committee and assures Jonas that they like the direction the renovation committee is taking. After almost four months of developing plans and convening student focus groups, the renovation committee takes the plans to the capital layout committee for final approval before groundbreaking. Following formal presentation of the plans, Stella begins asking questions about the plans, and Jonas begins to feel unsupported and blindsided. He feels that the questions she is asking could have been answered long before now and begins to get a sense that she has not read the plans until now.

- If you were Jonas, what would you do?
- How do you approach this situation given that Stella is your direct supervisor?
- How does Jonas leverage his relationship with Stella to move the plans forward?

AM I A STUDENT OR A PROFESSIONAL?

Andre is a new student activities director at State U, where he earned his undergraduate degree. This is also the same office he worked in during his last two undergraduate years as an office assistant. Andre left the university and earned his MA from a neighboring university. He has been gone from State U for three years while he finished his professional work.

Andre's new role comes with many responsibilities that are not new to him, but navigating the university as a professional is a bit different. He has been gone from State U for three years, but many of the same individuals are still in place from his undergraduate days. However, his direct supervisor, Ronda, the dean of students, has only been at State for six months.

During the search and interview process for the student activities director position, Ronda was torn between two candidates: Andre and another candidate. She ultimately recommended Andre to the vice president because of his charisma as well as his knowledge of and history with State U.

Five months into Andre's tenure, he was appointed as the Homecoming Committee chair for the university, a prestigious role at State because homecoming is a huge event for the university and surrounding community. Andre was elated and thrilled by this honor and began working as chair immediately. He knew he had the full support of Ronda, but was feeling tension with another colleague, Sarah. Sarah is the associate director of student activities and has been at the university for 20 years. She also directly reports to Andre.

With the preparations in full swing, it is clear that Sarah has little respect for Andre and his vision. She does everything she can to obstruct progress, including not following directions, missing meetings, and even calling her own meetings with other committee members at the same time.

Andre is becoming more and more frustrated with the process and lack of support. He is spending all of his time fixing Sarah's mistakes and lack of follow-through. He decides to talk to Ronda regarding Sarah's behavior. As he is meeting with Ronda and laying out what he is seeing and feeling, he realizes he sounds as if he is just complaining and directing blame. Ronda says to talk to Sarah and leaves Andre to resolve the situation. Feeling unsupported, Andre is unsure what to do.

- If you were Andre, what would you do?
- What kind of conversation should you have with Sarah?
- Discuss Ronda's reaction to Andre's dilemma.
- What kind of advice would you give to individuals in Andre's position who take professional jobs at their undergraduate institutions?

ARE YOU MY MENTOR OR NOT?

Jenna is a student affairs professional who has been working in her current role for six months. She enjoys the work and student interactions, but she is especially excited about the mentor she was assigned when she started working. She was assigned to Kent, the dean of students, who has a great reputation on campus and in the region for his mentoring of new professionals.

In her first month, she contacts Kent and they have coffee. He gives her all kinds of very practical advice about balance, navigating campus, and how her position fits into the larger organizational structure. They set up monthly meetings over coffee, and it has really helped Jenna to acclimate and understand her new position. At the five-month mark, the e-mails from Kent become short and Jenna interprets them as mean-spirited. Jenna senses something is not right and asks Kent about it. He says that everything is fine; he is just really busy and a little overwhelmed. She decides to lay off a bit and does not contact him for a few months.

At six months, she has a performance review with her supervisor, and she is asked how the mentoring relationship is going. She talks about how it started strong, but that she has not had contact with Kent in a couple of months. Judy, her supervisor, states that when she met with Kent last week, he said that Jenna seemed to lack follow-through, and he did not have tremendously positive things to say about her work thus far. Judy says that she will submit a marginal performance review, and if it doesn't improve in the next six months, she may be let go. Jenna is devastated and confused about why Kent would say those things.

- What should Jenna do?
- Should Jenna confront Kent about his comments to Judy? Think about the differential supervisory relationship in your response. How could that affect Jenna and her role at the university?
- Discuss why Judy told Jenna about the conversation with Kent. Do you think it was appropriate for Judy to disclose it to Jenna? Why or why not?

SHOULD I BE OFFENDED?

Robin and Min both work as associate directors in a transition office at State College. They were hired at the same time, five years ago, from the same graduate program in student affairs. While they work closely, they don't spend much time together socially, as they are at different stages in their personal lives.

The office is very excited because a new professional will be joining in a week. Troy is joining as a liaison to residential life and is the first new hire since Min and Robin were hired five years ago. The director, Kathy, has worked hard to find the funding and justification to hire another professional. The scope and impact of the programs the office provides to the campus community have been well documented.

As the office is preparing for Troy's arrival, the current staff members meet to discuss how they can help him make this transition.

Min says, "I think we should give him some materials and have him read for the first week or so."

Robin: "I understand where you're coming from; however, I also think we need to develop some one-on-one opportunities for him to talk to other professionals across campus. He's going to work closely with them, and sitting down to introduce himself and his new role would be important."

Kathy: "I like that idea; let's each come up with a list of people and we can meet again this afternoon to put a plan in place."

Later that afternoon at their meeting, Robin and Min both come with a list. Min has quite a long list and Robin has just a few names.

Kathy: "Okay, what do we have?"

Min: "Well, I wrote down each person I've worked with in the past few weeks and the major players who work on our programs."

Robin: "I just listed the important players. I decided he'll meet other folks later, but these are the most influential."

Min: "I think you need to qualify that. I'm looking at your list, and there are lots of folks I think will be very impactful, but they are not on this list."

Robin: "Well, if you understood what we actually do in this office, your list would look a bit different."

Min: "Wow, where did that come from?"

Kathy: "Okay, let's refocus here and get back to working with our lists to help Troy."

Robin: "I don't want to get back to the list. I want to talk about this. I feel like I clean up all kinds of stuff this office doesn't do, and it's getting old. Bringing a new person into the office and setting him up for failure isn't something I want to be part of."

Kathy: "Wow, where is this coming from? I'm not sure what you're talking about. I have a meeting in a few minutes but feel we really need to discuss this more. Clearly, I'm missing something. And from the expression on Min's face, she is as well."

- What are the major issues in this case? Discuss the issues from Robin's perspective, Min's perspective, and Kathy's perspective.
- How do the various perspectives differ?
- Kathy is the supervisor of this office. Explore her role and how she should begin to address this issue. Make a plan for Kathy to help establish a healthy working relationship for Min and Robin.
- What role does office politics and culture play in this case? How do you create a high-functioning culture in which everyone feels he or she has a voice?

LACKING LEADERSHIP

The office of judicial affairs at Bay College has overcome major leadership issues. The director resigned last year amid some controversy, and the office has had three failed searches following the resignation. The VP of student affairs comes to the next meeting and asks someone to step up as interim director. The role would be short term while the college reorganizes the entire student affairs structure, and with it, the judicial affairs office.

There are five professionals in the office. Three are new with fewer than two years of professional experience, leaving the other two as potential candidates for the interim position. Jillian and Rita together have fewer than 10 years of experience; however, neither is interested in taking on this interim role.

- What are the issues in this case? Explore the covert issues. What could be going on at Bay and in the student affairs division?
- Explore the issues of being associated, in a leadership role, with the judicial affairs office at Bay. What are the potential risks? What are the potential benefits?
- You are a consultant to the new internal interim director, either Jillian or Rita; how do you advise her and what do you focus on in the first 30 days, 100 days, and beyond?
- What are the political implications for both Jillian and Rita if they don't take the interim position? What are the implications for the judicial affairs office?

TAKE CONTROL OF THE BREAKS

Within the advising office at Evergreen University, the culture is collaborative and collegial. Advisors often bounce ideas off each other and use meeting time (formal and informal) to role-play difficult cases and discuss best practices. Lately, however, Bob, the director, has noticed the informal meetings taking place a lot more often. The advisors are using a common area, essentially, to take breaks and discuss personal issues. On Monday he decides to track the time the advisors spent "taking breaks," and finds that, in an eight-hour work day, they were on "break" for approximately two hours, not including their lunch break.

- What are the issues in this case?
- Informal processing is important and has always been valued at Evergreen. Develop a strategy for Bob to address this situation without micromanaging the professional advisors.

- Discuss how leaders influence culture and set tone. How does Bob find balance between being overbearing as a leader/manager and creating a positive and productive environment?

IS AN APOLOGY NECESSARY?

As the director of a unit, you are holding your annual opening session with your professional staff, a gathering of some 30 people. During a question-and-answer period toward the end of the meeting, one staff member challenges you on a particularly sticky new college policy affecting staff vacations. When the policy was introduced last spring, you opposed it in private meetings with your supervisor, and the staff is generally aware that you did. You cut off the offender with a flippant, sarcastic response, and the meeting ends with no further questions from staff. As you leave the meeting, it occurs to you that you may owe that staff member an apology. At the same time, you are reluctant to give him any satisfaction, because he consistently challenges limits on every policy matter and commonly assumes the role of rebel in every staff meeting.

- Should you apologize? If the offense was given in public, shouldn't the apology be made in public?
- What ethical principles should you consider?
- If you were the director and could replay the meeting, would you act differently? How do you think your department now feels about asking controversial questions in public settings?
- Have you ever been in a situation when your personal values or opinion conflicted with a decision that required your support? How did you handle this situation?

9

PERSONAL FOUNDATIONS

I CAN HANDLE IT

Kat is a new student affairs professional at Dylan College. Her department is responsible for campus activities and programming, and, full of new professionals, her office culture is highly energetic and fun.

During her first week on the job, she gravitates toward Alicia, who has worked at Dylan for the past six months. She is also a new professional and seems very nice. She helps Kat set up her office, contacts computer services, arranges for a campus tour, and helps Kat make connections around campus.

Two months into the job, Kat's supervisor assigns her a big, exciting project. Kat tells Alicia the good news, but Alicia seems taken aback by the announcement. Two weeks later Kat has a question related to the project that she is sure Alicia can answer. As Kat approaches Alicia, she overhears Alicia talking with another colleague. "I can't believe Kat. You know, she basically stole the project from me. She's really conniving and a suck-up. I suggest that you watch out for her. I thought we were friends. If that's the case, I'd hate to see how she treats her enemies."

- What are the issues in this case?
- Who are the key stakeholders?
- What are Kat's options and how might each one play out?
- Which course of action do you believe is the best? How should she proceed?
- Make an action plan for Kat to address this situation.

- Have you ever been in a situation similar to Kat's? What about Alicia's? Explain how you handled it. Did you ever feel misunderstood? How did you deal with the confusion?

COMPARING WORK ETHICS

Parent orientation is an involved, one-day program for parents of incoming freshmen. The orientation involves check-in, multiple information sessions, lunch, and a parent panel. Stephanie and Bill, both orientation coordinators, were asked by their supervisor to plan a parent orientation session on challenges facing today's college students. Stephanie and Bill's session will be one of the featured workshops. Two weeks before the event, the two meet to strategize for the session. Bill is very structured and wants to do some research on the topic. He envisions the session including a very detailed PowerPoint. He asks that they divide up the responsibilities and develop a timeline for accomplishing each task. Stephanie agrees but doesn't think the session is a big deal. She's presented on this topic before and has more of a "wing it" approach.

A week after their initial meeting, the two sit down to discuss their progress. While Bill has completed all the tasks on his list, Stephanie has not. She explains, "Bill, I've done this presentation before; I'll get it done. Don't worry. It'll be great." Bill leaves the meeting feeling concerned and frustrated. He decides to move forward and creates the PowerPoint and presentation outline. He shares this information with Stephanie; she thinks it's great and expresses her gratitude. The two facilitate the session and receive great feedback from the parents. Their supervisor congratulates them on an outstanding session. The next day Bill lunches with a colleague and expresses his frustration: "I did the whole thing! She didn't do anything but gets to share the credit. That just isn't fair! I can't believe our boss didn't reprimand her for slacking. Stephanie is unprofessional. She's a slacker." The colleague suggests that Bill talk with Stephanie; Bill replies, "I have to work with her. I don't want to upset her. I'll just deal with her."

- What are the issues in this case? Consider primary and secondary issues.

- There are two sides to every story. Would your opinion of Stephanie change if you knew that she was coordinating most of parents' weekend and felt overwhelmed?
- What is your reaction to Bill's confiding in a colleague? What if that colleague shared the story with others, thus damaging Stephanie's reputation on campus? What if Bill continued to talk behind Stephanie's back and shared his opinion with others on campus, thus damaging Stephanie's reputation on campus?
- Have you ever been in a situation where a colleague was speaking negatively about another colleague? How did you handle the situation?

WORKING AT YOUR ALMA MATER

After completing her bachelor's at Wisconsin Northern College, Allie was hired as an admissions counselor. In this capacity, she recruits potential students, attends college fairs, and coordinates on-campus visit days. Since Allie is a recent graduate, she is still close with many students on campus. Friday night Allie joined some of her undergraduate friends in the residence halls for a small gathering. Campus police knock on the door of the party and demand IDs. Some of the attendees are under age, and Allie's name goes into the police report. The dean of students is not her direct supervisor, but is her mentor. Allie was not drinking, but she was present. Monday morning Allie was waiting for the dean when he arrived on campus. After explaining the incident and apologizing, the dean responded, "I'm disappointed, but you made a mistake. Learn from it and move on." Allie's boss had a very different message. She said, "You'll never reach your goals if you continue with this behavior. You're now on probation."

- What is your reaction to Allie's behavior? Can you justify her actions? Why or why not?
- What is your reaction to how Allie handled the situation with her mentor and supervisor? How would you have handled the situation?
- What is your reaction to the way the dean and supervisor responded to Allie? If you were Allie's supervisor, how would you respond? What if this was not an isolated incident?

- In the actual case, Allie's supervisor continued to bring up the situation over the next three years. How should Allie handle these unwelcome reminders?

SMALL FISH IN A BIG POND

Fresh out of graduate school, Zion assumed a position as coordinator of student activities at a very small liberal arts college. In his position he wore many hats: he advised the student government and programming board; oversaw student activity fee allocation; facilitated leadership seminars; served as Greek advisor; wrote the student handbook; facilitated judicial hearings; and was liaison to career services, residence life, counseling services, and campus safety. After three years, Zion decided it was time to challenge himself and seek a position at a larger university. He was hired at a large, flagship university where his primary responsibilities were to oversee the student programming board and student fee allocation process. After overcoming his initial learning curve, Zion became bored and frustrated. Although his days were filled, he felt underused because his responsibilities were so limited. He had a lot of experience in many facets of student services.

- What suggestions do you have for Zion? Would your suggestions change if he were only in his current position for two months? One year?
- Zion has worked in two distinct institutional types. What recommendations do you have to help him transition from one type to another? What common mistakes do new professionals make when they move to another institution?
- Discuss positive ways to build a reputation within your institution. How might Zion establish himself as a professional on the university campus?

NEGOTIATING PUNISHMENT

Jeremy, a residence hall director, connects well with students, who find him approachable, likeable, and trustworthy. He even plays on many intramural sports teams. Students regularly seek advice from Jeremy and many consider him a friend, in addition to their hall director/advisor. One night, two members from the intramural team are found smoking pot in their residence hall room. Jeremy is the judicial officer assigned to the case. In the judicial meeting, the two students beg Jeremy not to notify their parents. They promise that the pot smoking was a "one-time thing" and promise not to get into trouble again. Jeremy knows these are "good" guys and feels obligated to give them a second chance. Wanting to maintain his rapport with the students, Jeremy issues a sanction, and then tells the two on the side that he will cut their punishment in half if they can beat him at a game of racquetball.

- What is your initial reaction to Jeremy's sanctioning? Discuss why Jeremy handled the situation the way he did.
- Argue the pros and cons to his strategy. Regarding his approach to this violation, are there any potential consequences he should consider?
- How would you handle the situation? Role-play.

NEGATIVITY IS CONTAGIOUS

Sheila, a new member of the student affairs team, is eager and excited to assume her first professional position. During the interview process, a couple of staff members referred to the challenges faced by the department, but her desire to join the department outweighed any concerns raised during the interview. The first week of her new job, Sheila lunched with some of her more seasoned colleagues. Over the course of the conversation, they complained about many aspects of their department, including their ambiguous job descriptions, unclear direction, and lack of supervision. Sheila didn't let their comments bring her down; a naturally optimistic person, she simply listened. Over the next few months, many members of the department continued to speak negatively about it, which created a contentious, adversarial culture within the department. Behind closed doors, this faction complained about every decision and continued to question authority. Sheila's optimistic attitude started to wane and she found herself getting sucked into the negativity. She went from being really positive and happy to miserable. She knows she's not making a good impression, but staff members keep feeding the negativity. When she tried to find a silver lining or question their negativity, her colleagues became upset and isolated her as the "goody-goody."

- Discuss the organizational culture. How is culture built and changed?
- What are Sheila's options in the long and short term? Discuss the benefits and challenges of each option.
- How might Sheila have prevented this negative first-year experience? Discuss how to approach the hiring process and various strategies for determining a good fit.

I REALLY WANT THAT JOB

Marianna has lived and worked far away from her family for the past six years. She really misses them and wants to move. What appears to be the perfect job opens up at the community college close to where her parents and siblings live. Extremely excited, Marianna applies for the position and is granted an interview. During the interview she asks appropriate, tough questions: "What are your likes and frustrations? Explain the culture of your department. Do people get along and socialize outside of work? What is it like to work for the supervisor? What keeps you here?"

While she really wants the job, her inner voice is telling her that there are some serious issues in this department. Staff members do not appear to like each other, they work long hours, and the institution is undergoing major cutbacks. A sense of foreboding resonated throughout her interview.

- Discuss Marianna's dilemma. Often when we want something, we convince ourselves that the reality is not as bad as we think. How might Marianna convince herself that this will be a good move?
- If offered the position, should Marianna accept it? Why or why not? If she does, what should she consider?
- Have you ever talked yourself into something that later turned out to be a mistake? Discuss. What lessons did you learn from that experience?

SINGLE IN STUDENT AFFAIRS

Mark and Susan are new to the department. They spend a great deal of time together during and outside of work. Since they are both new to the area, neither has any friends. Since they don't know anyone else, they find comfort and companionship with each other. The department has strict rules about not dating colleagues, but everyone senses something is brewing between them.

- How do you handle the situation if you are Mark or Susan?
- How do you handle the situation if you supervise Mark and Susan?
- What are the pros and cons of coworkers dating?

THAT E-MAIL WASN'T MEANT FOR EVERYONE

The vice president of student affairs recently disseminated an all-division e-mail discussing a realignment plan for various offices. With pending budget cuts, realignment and reduction of staff have been rumored for the past six months. Understandably, most staff members are on edge about losing their jobs and are actively seeking employment elsewhere. The VP's recent e-mail only confirmed everyone's suspicion. Since many department chairs had already shared the news three days earlier, the e-mail seemed trite and late. Suzanne forwarded the e-mail and her comments to her "best" work friend. She commented on the delay of the e-mail and questioned the necessity of the pending restructuring. After hitting send, she realized that rather than send the e-mail to her friend, she had sent it to the division. Suzanne begins to panic.

- What should Suzanne do immediately? Eventually? Discuss her options and the pros and cons of each one.
- Discuss the "dos and don'ts" of e-mail etiquette. What are some common mistakes people make regarding e-mail? How is tone translated via e-mail? How do you ensure the professionalism of your e-mails?

- Do any of the discussion points from the previous bullet point translate to social media? How, if at all, is social media different? How does social media play a role, if at all, at work?

DATING THE BOSS

Emilia has been a hall director for the past three years. During this time, she developed an intimate relationship with her supervisor, Paul, the assistant director of residence life. To avoid a conflict of interest, Sam, the director of residence life, now directly supervises Emilia. Although the reporting structures have changed, problems still ensue. Among her hall director peers, Emilia is no longer seen as a confidante. Her peers fear that anything they tell her about their frustrations at work will get back to their boss, Paul. As a result, there is little conversation in hall director meetings, during staff lunches, or among the group in general.

- What are the issues in this case? What are your suggestions for resolving the problem(s)? What are the advantages and disadvantages of each option?
- Discuss the dynamic created when coworkers date. Have you ever been in this situation? How did the relationship affect, if at all, the work culture?

PASSING THE REINS

Georgia is the associate dean of students. She recently went on maternity leave and asked the coordinator of student activities, Josie, to advise the student government association (SGA) in her absence. Calvin, the president of SGA, comes to Josie's third meeting intoxicated. Some of the student representatives make jokes about his state, but this seems to be a common occurrence that the students find humorous. When Josie approached Calvin after the meeting, he denied drinking. He claimed he was just goofing off.

Not sure what to do, Josie approached her interim supervisor, the dean of students. The dean told her he would handle the situation and speak with Calvin. Josie suspects that the talk never happened when Calvin showed up for the next meeting intoxicated again.

- What are the major issues in this case? What are Josie's options for handling the situation with Calvin? What are the pros and cons of each option?
- How does Josie handle the dean? Discuss her options and the possible consequences of each option. What if Josie is wrong, and the dean did talk with Calvin?

DO YOU NEED HELP?

Ken is the vice president of student affairs at Free State College. He is a beloved VP, both on campus and nationally. He has been at Free State for seven years and has won numerous national and campus-based awards for his contributions to student affairs and development. Aran is a new student affairs professional at Free State and took the job for the opportunity to work with Ken.

Five weeks after Aran joined the college, Ken stops by Aran's office to see how things are going. Aran tells him that things are going great, that he feels very welcomed and included in the unit and is really enjoying the students. As Ken is leaving, he tells Aran to call if he needs anything and that he is always available. A week later, Aran receives an e-mail about the new online submission process to request space for programs. He finds the e-mail a bit confusing, but chalks it up to his being new. He could call Ken, but it seems quite trivial, and feels as though he shouldn't bug Ken with this. Later that same day he is opening his mail and sees a notice that a renewal needs to be filed for a grant that funds a recreational sports club and its activities. Again not sure what do to, Aran puts the notice in a pile and decides not to bug Ken with it.

Two weeks later, Aran gets a call from the director of the union inform-ing him that some of the student groups are not using the new online request system and that they need to start using it to secure space from now on. A week later, a very upset student president is in Aran's office stating that his group has no space for a comedian who's coming to campus tomorrow. Five minutes later, 12 students from a recreational sports club are standing at Aran's door because their equipment is being removed from the field house because they didn't comply with their grant. Aran is devastated—how could things go so badly so fast?

- What should Aran do? What is his responsibility to the students? To Ken? To the institution?
- Develop a supervision plan for Aran. How can you help him be successful at Free State?

FINDING BALANCE—I NEED TO EAT?

Matt is a perfectionist and a bit of a self-defined overachiever. He is one year into his first supervisory position as director of academic advising in an office with 12 professional advisors and two office staff. The office staff members handle all appointments and student scheduling. The student-to-advisor ratio is 800:1. When Matt saw this, he quickly offered to take some of the load off of his colleagues and advise some students.

The workload ebbs and flows throughout the year, and during registration times, February to April, the office is very busy. The rest of the year is steady but manageable. As January ends and February begins, Matt is curious about his first registration period. The appointments start to fill on his schedule and he quickly notices that if he doesn't manually block off time to eat, the office staff will set up appointments when they see an opening. At first he sees this as being a team player so he doesn't say much. By the end of month one of crazy advising, Matt is exhausted but still feels he can't say anything because the entire office is busy. Besides, he can always eat when he gets home.

- Discuss the issues of this case. Do you see any problems with Matt's behavior?
- What does Matt's behavior say about role modeling and mentoring?
- Develop a plan for Matt; how can he get this behavior under control and be an effective team player and leader?

MY NAME IS PENNY

Penny is associate director of recreation services at Pummel College and has worked in this position for five years. She has 10 supervisees and takes great pride in knowing all of their names, family members' names, and a great deal about their personal lives. She is a strong believer in the value of relationships and feels that when she knows about her colleagues, she is a better supervisor and colleague.

John, vice president of student life, has been at Pummel for 25 years. He has had a great career at Pummel and is very well respected around campus. Penny does not report to John directly but has done quite a bit of work with him over the past five years. Each time John sees Penny, she is pretty sure that he is calling her "Pammie," but she has never corrected him. It has been years since he first called her "Pammie," and she thinks it may look a little silly to correct him now. In Penny's eyes, it has never been an issue because he has not had to introduce her in a large group.

Fall semester at Pummel College was exciting because a group of international scholars was visiting to look at student life and spend some time with the unit. Penny had met the group when she was visiting with them last year. She wasn't responsible for the visit but had been e-mailing some of the delegates about their visit. As the visit was getting closer, Penny was excited, even though she was also extremely busy with both an upcoming accreditation visit and fall sports events in the rec center. With all of her activities, Penny lost track of the upcoming international team visit.

On Monday morning, she opens her e-mail and sees one from one of her international colleagues whom she was sure was visiting Pummel College. The first line states, "It was a great visit to Pummel; however, I was sad that I was not able to spend any time with you during our visit. Thank you for your hard work and I hope to see you on future visit."

Penny was dumbfounded. How could she have been cut out of the visit? She was so enraged she called Pat in the Student Life Office to find out what happened. Pat said, "You weren't on the list and I wasn't sure why. I asked John and he looked a little confused but proceeded on." All of a sudden it hit Penny that John thinks her name is Pammie, not Penny: "Oh, my gosh, what have I done? I might as well just quit. How do you tell someone he's called you the wrong name for five years? What an idiot I am!"

- How should Penny proceed?
- Does Penny have bigger problems with self-esteem and security?
- Should she quit her job? Why or why not?

I WILL WAIT

Brenda and the seven other academic advisors who work exclusively with athletes decide to go out for a drink after a long week of orientation. The group consists of young professionals whom Brenda supervises during orientation but not during the regular academic year. The college has decentralized advising, and each advisor reports to an academic dean during the traditional fall and winter semesters.

The group is having a blast and decides to go to a dance club. Brenda isn't sure she wants to go dancing, but she's not quite ready to go home. She decides to stay and wait for Ron while he takes the group to the dance club. The group intends to take a taxi home when they finish.

As the group leaves, Brenda moves to the bar so she can grab one more drink and not occupy a table by herself. She sits at the bar and suddenly the bartender hands her another drink compliments of the gentleman at the end of the bar. She looks over and sees a young man waving to her. She smiles and he moves to sit next to her. There is something a little familiar about the young man, but Brenda is unable to place him. They begin talking and he tells her all about a big trip he intends to take this summer and how excited he is to go back to school in the fall. He never says where he attends college, but Brenda never asks, either. Just as they are getting into a nice conversation, Ron comes in and asks if she is ready to go. Ron sees the gentleman sitting with Brenda and shakes his hand, saying, "Have a good night, Luke, and see you in the fall." When they get in the car, Brenda asks how Ron knew his name, and why he was going to see him in the fall.

Ron said that Luke is one of their new star athletes. He'll be a sophomore in the fall and plans to play lacrosse. Brenda is dumbfounded; he never told her he was attending college in town nor did he disclose that he is a student athlete.

Even worse, he's underage and only a second-year student. The school has a strict off-campus code of conduct for students, and especially student athletes. Underage drinking is not a zero-tolerance offense, but is taken very seriously.

- What should Brenda do?
- If Ron had not said anything, Brenda would never know about Luke. Does that change her responsibility to the school or her profession?

COINCIDENCE, PATTERNS, OR SHOULD WE BE ALARMED?

Tom is a new professional in the student affairs office at Speedy University. He has been in the role for almost a year, and is beginning to feel comfortable with the work and the university. Helena is his direct supervisor and has been a great mentor for him.

Even though Tom has been working in the office for nearly a year, he feels he doesn't know Helena very well. She is so dynamic in her work role but very quiet about her personal life. He also knows she commutes about an hour to campus every day, but has no idea whether she has a partner, children, or any hobbies.

At lunch every day Helena walks the campus as part of her daily routine. On Monday Tom decides to join Helena to see if he can get to know her any better. Helena is quite surprised that Tom asks and even seems somewhat annoyed. They walk for about 20 minutes and Tom senses she is not enjoying the company. He makes an excuse that he needs something from the bookstore and will meet her back at the office. Tom is thinking, "Well, I tried, but something is not quite right about Helena." He is confused how someone can be so dynamic and engaging when the topic is just work, but so closed off and irritated when the conversation gets personal.

Back at the office, Tom is finishing up a project when he notices Helena packing up her stuff; he thinks this is strange because it's only 2:00 p.m. and she always stays much later. He pops into her office and notices that she is crying. He immediately asks what's wrong and whether he can help with anything. She dismisses him quite abruptly and says she has an emergency she must take care of and will be back in the morning.

The next day Helena is already in the office when Tom arrives. He stops by her office. She seems to be in good spirits and goes over some details for the meeting with the dean of students about their upcoming program. Tom looks at Helena, and as soon as he makes eye contact, she looks away very quickly. He looks again and notices what he thinks is a bruise on her cheek. He also notices her fingernails are chewed down to nothing. This is odd because Helena always has nicely polished and manicured nails. He asks what's up, not mentioning what he thinks he's seeing. She says all is well.

Later that day, Tom hears what he thinks is yelling coming from behind the building. The office has a delivery door that backs up to a loading dock and alley. He notices that the door is ajar and opens it to see what's going on. Helena is standing on the loading dock, fighting with a man. Tom isn't sure what to do as they don't see him and are clearly engaged in a serious fight. Suddenly Helena pushes the man backward and he grabs her by the hair and punches her in the stomach. The man then gets into a parked car and takes off, leaving Helena on the loading dock. Before Helena can see Tom, he goes back into the office and begins filling his water bottle. Five minutes later, Helena comes in through the door and seems a bit startled to see him. She quickly goes into work mode and talks about an idea for an upcoming event. She tells Tom to think about the idea and maybe they can meet later to discuss it further. She then goes back to her office.

- What are the issues of this case?
- Tom suspects that someone is abusing Helena. He witnessed a fight and has lots of anecdotal evidence and feelings about the situation. Where should he go for advice and guidance?
- Explore and discuss this case from a supervisor-supervisee perspective. What are the implications of the relationship? Develop a plan for Tom to help Helena. What may this mean for Tom and his future at Speedy University?

WINTER PARTY GONE BADLY

Gene is the associate dean of first-year programs and often opens his home for holiday parties. The winter holiday party has become quite an event, and he is pleased that those in attendance include seasoned and new professionals at various levels across campus.

This year there are three new professionals in the first-year programs office. Bryn, Richard, and Ignacio all joined within the last six months and have yet to attend the winter party. All three go to Sabrina, the associate director, to get a sense of the party, dress, gifts, and other details to help them as it appears this is quite the social event. Sabrina gives a nice overview, but leaves them with a warning about overindulging in alcohol. She says, "This party is a very nice event and people are watching. The VP will be there, as well as other influential people from across campus. Just watch yourself and don't drink too much."

Bryn, Richard, Ignacio, and Sabrina all decide to go as a group. They arrive at the party, and see that Gene and his partner have gone overboard this year. Their home is beautifully decorated, there are party favors for each guest, and everyone seems to be in an incredibly festive mood. As the evening wears on, Bryn is finding herself quite bored and asks Richard if he wants to take a tour of the home. They ask Gene for permission and he readily agrees. The home is just stunning and it is apparent that they took great care and effort in decorating. As they head downstairs, they find a number of the career services folks hanging out in the downstairs living room. Ignacio is among them. As they begin talking to the group, it is evident that Ignacio is quite intoxicated.

Bryn and Richard try to pull him away but he insists he is fine. They go to find Sabrina to see if they can get him out of there before he gets any drunker. She agrees and they head back downstairs to tell him it's time to go. Ignacio becomes quite belligerent, as do many of the other career services folks. "I am not leaving. You're not my boss," yells Ignacio.

"I think it would be a good idea, but if you want to stay we're going to head home," Sabrina replies. Sabrina, Bryn, and Richard decide there isn't much they can do, and Ignacio is an adult. So, they leave the party.

In the car on the way home, Bryn says, "I feel kind of bad. Should we have at least warned someone else who wasn't so drunk about the people in the basement?"

"Not much we can do. They're all grown-ups," responds Richard.

Monday, when they all get to work, they find Gene talking with one of the office staff about the party. "I think next year we may have to go to an alcohol-free party. I can't have this behavior happening at my house any more. This used to be such a nice event. I'm not sure what to do about it. It was just out of control this year."

Sabrina asks Gene, "What happened? I thought the party was lovely."

"You must have left before Ignacio and the career services staff decided my basement was a bar. They spilled alcohol all over the furniture, had a pillow fight and broke a vase, and someone threw up in the basement bathtub and never told us. It was a mess. You're his supervisor. I think he needs a good talking-to. Sabrina, take care of it."

- What are the issues in this case?
- Analyze the case from Sabrina's perspective. What approach should she take? How does an off-campus party affect work culture?
- What advice would you give to Gene about future events?

ATHLETES ARE TREATED DIFFERENTLY

Jonah is a packaging major and a student athlete at a Division I university. He's a very good student and an accomplished athlete. During one of his core classes, the professor is doing a test review for the upcoming mid-term exam. Jonah raises his hand and asks a clarifying question.

The response he gets from the professor is shocking. The faculty member goes off on a tangent about how "ignorant and privileged" student athletes are. He goes on to say, "Student athletes dictate the rules for everyone, and that special treatment will no longer be awarded in this class." Jonah is confused as he has never asked for special treatment and believes he is earning an A in the course. Unsure what to do, he makes an appointment with the director of student athlete support services to find out how to report this faculty member, while also avoiding retribution from him.

- What are the issues in this case?
- Explore Jonah's options for addressing the faculty member.
- Explore the larger campus issues regarding the perception of student athletes. How do you begin to address those issues?

STUDENT LEARNING AND DEVELOPMENT

IF SHE GOES, I GO

The Department of Residence Life has a probation policy for resident advisors. If they receive a 2.5 GPA for two consecutive semesters, they are on probation. If their cumulative GPA falls below a 2.5, the RA is dismissed. RA Sheila receives a 2.45 for the fall semester, but maintains a 2.6 GPA. Over winter break, Sheila calls Mark, her supervisor, to discuss her grades and express her concern that she might be fired. Mark double-checks the policy and assures Sheila that she will not be fired but that she needs to raise her GPA for spring semester to be rehired for the following academic year. Still concerned, Sheila makes Mark promise that she will not lose her job for spring semester. Toward the start of spring semester, RA grades are checked. Christina, the director of residence life, contacts Mark via e-mail to express her concerns regarding Sheila:

> Mark, I am very concerned with Sheila's fall grades. She obviously isn't putting her academics first. If I let her stay on staff spring semester, she'll need some serious supervision. Please meet with me at 9 a.m. to discuss this issue.

Mark is furious. He decides that if Christina fires Sheila, he will quit.

- What is the best-case scenario? Worst-case scenario? What would you do to bring about the best case?

- What might happen if Mark enters the meeting confrontationally? What if he enters collaboratively with Sheila's best interests at heart?
- What do you think is Christina's intention? Why do you think Mark responded so negatively to the e-mail? Do you think his initial reaction is appropriate?
- Rather than inquire and listen, we often make assumptions about people's intentions. Has either Mark or Christina made unnecessary assumptions? In a work setting, have you ever incorrectly assumed something about another person? How did you resolve the situation? What did you learn from making an assumption?

WHAT DO YOU DO ALL DAY?

Rena is a graduate assistant in Greek Affairs at Corner U. Her role is making sure that the organizations have filed all paperwork at the national level and monitoring grades of Greek students. She is required to work 20 hours a week and also attends class in the master's program at Corner. You are John, and you supervise Rena, two other GAs, and five professional staff members. As a new professional, you are working hard to find a balance between giving your supervisees autonomy and making sure the work is getting done.

Rena is always in the office as required and appears to be very busy. She is often meeting with Greek students and collaborating with others in the office. While she appears very busy, you begin to see a pattern of work not being submitted and paperwork not being filed. You ask her for a project timeline regarding the submission of paperwork to the national office. She does not respond, so you follow up. Following the third e-mail, you pay a visit to Rena's office. She tells you that she will get it to you. Following that meeting you find out that she failed to submit a report to a national chapter, and it has contacted you. You quickly fill out the report and submit it but now have to deal with Rena and her work.

- What do you do?
- How do you help Rena get her work done without micromanaging her?
- Discuss how you can be developmental and an effective supervisor simultaneously.

DO SOMETHING ABOUT IT

You are Rebecca, the director of a career center. As director, you supervise seven graduate assistants who advise and develop programs for the academic colleges on campus. You have noticed that the GAs are coming to you with complaints about one another; they report work not getting done, dress code violations, long lunches, not filing paperwork correctly, personal phone calls at work, and many other issues that seem to show an eroding professional culture in the office.

- Help Rebecca address these issues.
- Develop a professional plan to address the complaints and office culture.

MORE PROFESSIONAL CONFERENCES

Romie is a mid-level student affairs professional at Braymore. Braymore is known for its high levels of support for professional development, and its student affairs professionals are always adequately represented at state, regional, and national conferences. Romie has great interest in attending educational conferences and often takes part in opportunities. During her first year on the job, she attended eight conferences to help her learn her job and get a broader sense of student affairs.

Braymore just hired George, a new senior student affairs officer, who is instituting a new policy for professional travel. The policy is in development, but it has already created quite a buzz on campus. Individuals across campus are worried about funding and continued support for professional development activities. The new policy is published; the biggest changes involve reporting how the educational conference contributes to the success of Braymore students. Romie is fine with this change until George sends her a memo stating that she cannot attend any conferences for two years because she went to so many during her first year.

- Talk about the issues of fairness to Romie. How would you feel if you were Romie, and what would you do about it?

- What implications does this have for George's reputation as he begins his tenure at Braymore?
- How does this contribute to or create obstacles for policy development at Braymore?

SERVICE-LEARNING AND RELIGIOUS CONFLICTS

John works for Tuten College, a small, private, religiously affiliated college in a rural area of the United States. At Tuten, John is responsible for service-learning and outreach and placing students in positions. His students find placements all over the country. One of his students has found a placement working with an organization that assists pregnant women who have been raped and are seeking abortions. The organization provides funding and support following the procedure. As a religiously affiliated school, the university has taken a strong stand on abortion and the belief that life begins at conception. You know the student well and believe this is a great placement for her. Upon consultation with your dean, you find out that if she takes the placement, not only will she not earn credit for the service-learning course, but she also could be dismissed from the college.

- What should John do?
- What rights does the young woman have?

ALTERNATIVE BREAK GONE BADLY

Rory is the supervisor of alternative break at Upper College and is supervising 15 undergraduate students on a three-week international trip. The group is working on building a new school in a region that was destroyed during a recent tsunami. After four days, Rory notices that the students seem annoyed by many of the local citizens and even begin making up rude and offensive nicknames for them.

- What are the issues in this case?
- What kind of intervention should Rory have with her students during the trip?

- What kind of discussion should Rory have when the group returns to campus?
- Develop an ongoing plan to help Rory prepare students for future trips. How can she use this trip to learn techniques for future trips?

COMMUNITY STANDARDS

The students in Casey Hall at Owens University have developed strong community standards for the hall. They are part of the development and implementation process. On the fifth floor, the residents of one room requested a roommate change early in the year, but the resident assistant denied the request because it violated the community standards. The residence life professionals work hard to maintain the standards, while also meeting the students' safety and developmental needs. After three denied requests from the fifth-floor roommates to switch roommates, the students decide to call the president to complain about the community standards.

- What are the issues in this case?
- At what point should Casey Hall residence life staff decide to modify rules? What message does that send?
- Discuss what message modifying the rules and standards sends to students.

THE INTERRUPTION

Although you've asked her not to, your receptionist calls you in the middle of a student appointment. She anxiously explains that Barry, another one of your advisees, is on the phone and demanding to speak to you. He is using foul language and being very abusive to her. He wants to schedule an appointment with you tomorrow so he can register for next semester. As this is a very busy advising time of year, you are booked for the next two weeks. You remember that Barry had made three appointments with you earlier in the semester and didn't show up for any of them. Barry is from a prominent family at your school, and you feel that he tries to use this to his advantage. You believe that if you make special accommodations for his poor behavior, you will be reinforcing it.

- How should you handle the immediate situation? In the next few days? Do you ask the receptionist to speak with him, or do you speak with him? What about the student waiting in your office?
- Does this situation lend itself to a "teachable moment" for Barry? Explain. How do you balance customer service and student development?

MEDICAL DOCUMENTATION

Darnell, one of your advisees, has asked you to support a petition allowing him to withdraw retroactively from a previous semester due to medical problems. Darnell's grades that semester were abysmal. He explains his problems to you and provides medical documentation to back up his story. His case is strong enough, based on the medical documentation alone, that a review committee grants him the retroactive withdrawal. Several weeks later, while having lunch in the student union building, you overhear Darnell telling some students that he really fooled you and the college by making up a story and creating false medical documentation. He tells them the real reason he failed most of his classes is that he partied too much. Darnell doesn't know that you overheard his conversation.

- What are the options for addressing this situation? What are the advantages and disadvantages of each? Should this issue go beyond Darnell?
- Consider Darnell's development. Which option is the best to help him and his development?
- What specific steps should you take to resolve the situation?

SHY STUDENT

Will is a highly recruited African American freshman for the High State University basketball team. He stands 6 feet, 10 inches and despite his intimidating stature, is very shy and soft-spoken. Will has been enjoying his first semester at High State and has been preparing for the basketball season. Around mid-terms, Will has a meeting with his English professor to discuss coursework and progress. The professor explains to Will that his work has been unsatisfactory and that "his kind" should find classes that are not so difficult. The professor continues to go on a rant filled with racial and ethnic slurs as well as demeaning comments about student athletes. Will is appalled at the professor's words but does not say anything at the time for fear of getting a lower grade. Will is unsure how to address this situation and decides to see Angela, the academic success coach for student athletes.

- What are the issues in this case?
- Where does Angela begin addressing the issues in this case?
- Develop a plan for Angela to work with Will. Pay attention to the fact that Will is shy and soft-spoken.
- What other professionals should be involved in the discussions as Angela and Will work through the issues?

II

PRACTICAL ADVICE FOR
NEW PROFESSIONALS

When we interviewed new and seasoned professionals for this book, many offered advice, suggestions, and words of wisdom for other new professionals. While this is not an exhaustive list, their recommendations, sage counsel, and guided warnings may be useful to other new professionals.

- Look for something in anything.
- Especially for extroverts, who think out loud, think before you speak. People judge you initially by your verbal contributions. Make sure your comments are informed and thoughtful and respect the history and culture of your organization.
- When you start out, you need to be more of a follower. You are no longer a student leader, and you do not have the ear of the vice president or president. Know your place and respect the chain of command.
- While you might have been a well-respected student leader, as a new professional, you start from scratch. You have to establish your reputation as a hard worker, innovative thinker, and team player.
- Put in the time to understand the culture and politics of your organization. Spend time listening and asking questions. Understanding the cultural dynamics of your department, division, and college or university takes time. Learn the traditions, myths, rituals, and stories that make your campus unique.

- Keep your mouth shut. People will share sensitive information with you. Don't disclose what was intended to be private. Once you release information, even to a trusted source, you no longer control the facts. Privileged information should remain privileged.
- Know who is in the room. Every meeting, conversation, or casual encounter is an opportunity to network. Introduce yourself and make sincere connections.
- Join a diverse array of campus-wide committees throughout the first five years of your career. Be a positive, contributing member of each committee.
- Don't overstep your boundaries. Know your role and responsibilities.
- Authenticity is valuable. While you want to be known as a team player, work to move out of the "I want to please" mode. Please by doing great work and being authentic.
- Make your own decisions and think for yourself. Supervisors appreciate those who take the initiative and handle problems that are within their authority.
- While autonomy and initiative are valuable traits, always know when to inform your supervisor.
- Your supervisor defines your success. Clarify expectations and keep communication lines open.
- If you want to be a professional, dress professionally.
- Be prepared to do administrative paperwork; it's part of every job and is beneath no one.
- Be willing to change. Adapt as you find yourself. You can change your style mid-year.
- Admit mistakes and move on. Always tell the truth, especially if you've made a mistake. Mistakes happen. You want to be the one to break the news.
- Seek out your own professional development opportunities. Not all departments dedicate time and resources to professional development. Look to state, regional, and national associations to continue your professional development. You might also stay abreast of trainings and events on campus. Many human resource offices offer employee training in a variety of topics.
- Know who you are and what you stand for. Once you have this awareness, stretch yourself.

- Find and develop mentoring relationships. Remember that your supervisor isn't always your mentor. If this is the case, seek out others at your institution or within your professional association. Seek out someone in the division with some history and tenure to serve as your de facto mentor for insider information and perspective. Make sure it is someone you respect and trust.
- Your job is not the end-all and be-all. When your well-being is in jeopardy, you should leave.
- You need to stay as late as your supervisor and preferably come in before him or her.
- While you need to have high expectations for students, you also need to remember student development theory and meet them where they are.
- Never drink with or in front of students!
- You don't have to work 80 hours if you're effective and hard-working during your 40 hours.
- Impress everyone—students, supervisors, parents, support staff, and custodians. All are important people who deserve your respect.
- Humor can go a long way to relieve fear and embarrassment.
- Maintain professional boundaries with students. You are their advisor/supervisor, not their friend. If you need a friend, get a pet.
- Maintaining a social life outside of work is important. You often live, eat, work out, and so on, with students. You need your own life that does not include them. Do something outside of work that you're also passionate about.
- Learn as much as you can about campus resources. Being able to refer students to these resources will prove helpful.
- Master "breaking-in" strategies. Get to know the people and the rhythm of your new workplace. Avoid making a big splash too soon. No one wants to hear how you "used to do things" at your old school.
- Stay current! Stay abreast of current events and national higher education conversations through the *Chronicle of Higher Education*, *Inside Higher Ed*, and other publications. We also recommend attending professional conferences. While the school may not fund your participation, it's a good investment in your professional future and is tax-deductible.

- Complaining or having a poor attitude reflect negatively on you. People want to work with positive people. Avoid blaming others.
- Be judicious with technology. When in meetings, you should not be texting, e-mailing, or checking your social media sites.
- Conflict can be challenging. Seek first to understand, then to be understood.
- The student affairs field and your institution are way too small to burn bridges.
- Don't inherit other people's feuds. Form your own judgments of others.
- You won't be rewarded for merely doing your job—but be competent at it before branching out.
- Write for publication—formal and informal.
- Submit conference presentation proposals.
- Learn your physical and mental limits at work.
- Eat right, get enough sleep, and exercise. We tell students this all the time, but modeling such behavior benefits them and us.
- You don't need to do everything for everyone. You need to prove yourself, work hard, and be a team player, but you don't need to sacrifice your own personal well-being. Downtime is important to avoid burnout.
- Draw a clear line between personal and professional relationships. Your coworkers and supervisors will serve as references. You need to maintain positive professional boundaries.
- Learn the vernacular of the university. If you don't understand an acronym, ask!
- You need to reflect deeply on your own biases and level of privilege. Your interactions with students will be based on your personal experiences and perceptions. We make sense of the world based on our own experiences and how we interpret them. Knowing yourself and your prejudices is important.
- Determine which events you should attend versus which ones are mandatory. Get a sense of when your presence is important and when it's optional.

INDEX

*Titles of cases are in **boldface**.*

Several cases can lead to a deeper discussion about how a student leader fits in the larger college community because they clearly suggest the involvement of college and university staff and officials.

Each case comes with suggested discussion questions, beginning by asking participants to identify the issues in the case. The depth of questions often correlates to the complexity of the dilemma presented. Questions move beyond the specific case's basic issues to larger questions, making the cases adaptable to varying types of institutions, organizations, or situations."

—The Review of Higher Education

Sty/us

22883 Quicksilver Drive
Sterling, VA 20166-2102

Subscribe to our e-mail alerts: www.Styluspub.com

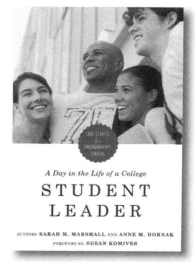